Shakespeare on the Double!™

D0169756

Othello

Shakespeare on the Double!™

Othello

translated by

Mary Ellen Snodgrass

WILEY

Wiley Publishing, Inc.

For general information on our other products and services or to obtain technical support please contact our Customer Care Department within the U.S. at (800) 762-2974, outside the U.S. at (317) 572-3993 or fax (317) 572-4002.

Wiley also publishes its books in a variety of electronic formats. Some content that appears in print may not be available in electronic books. For more information about Wiley products, please visit our web site at www.wiley.com.

Library of Congress Cataloging-in-Publication Data:
Shakespeare, William, 1564–1616.
  Othello / translated by Mary Ellen Snodgrass.
      p. cm. — (Shakespeare on the double!)
  Original text with parallel modern English translation.
  ISBN-13: 978-0-470-21275-2
  ISBN-10: 0-470-21275-6
  1. Othello (Fictitious character)—Drama. 2. Jealousy—Drama. 3. Venice (Italy)—Drama. 4. Cyprus—Drama. I. Snodgrass, Mary Ellen. II. Title.
  PR2829.A1 2008
  822.3'3—dc22

                                    2008001315

Printed in the United States of America

10 9 8 7 6 5 4 3 2 1

Book design by Melissa Auciello-Brogan
Book production by Wiley Publishing, Inc. Composition Services

Contents

ACT V

About the Translator

Mary Ellen Snodgrass is an award-winning author of textbooks and general reference works and a former columnist for the *Charlotte Observer*. A member of Phi Beta Kappa, she graduated magna cum laude from the University of North Carolina at Greensboro and Appalachian State University and holds degrees in English, Latin, psychology, and education of gifted children.

Introduction

*S*hakespeare on the Double! *Othello* provides the full text of the Bard's play side by side with an easy-to-read modern English translation that you can understand. You no longer have to struggle wondering what exactly "I kissed thee ere I killed thee" means! You can read the Shakespearean text on the left-hand pages and check the right-hand pages when Shakespeare's language stumps you. Or you can read only the translation, which enables you to understand the action and characters without struggling through the Shakespearean English. You can even read both, referring back and forth easily between the original text and the modern translation. Any way you choose, you can now fully understand every line of the Bard's masterpiece!

We've also provided you with some additional resources:

- **Brief synopsis** of the plot and action offers a broad-strokes overview of the play.
- **Comprehensive character list** covers the actions, motivations, and characteristics of each major player.
- **Visual character map** displays who the major characters are and how they relate to one another.
- **Cycle of death** pinpoints the sequence of deaths in the play, including who dies, how they die, and why they die.
- **Reflective questions** help you delve even more into the themes and meanings of the play.

Reading Shakespeare can be slow and difficult. No more! With *Shakespeare on the Double! Othello,* you can read the play in language that you can grasp quickly and thoroughly.

Synopsis

ACT I

Scene 1

On a street in the city-state of Venice, Italy, Roderigo, a Florentine noble, argues with Iago, the Moorish general's flag bearer. Roderigo, who loves the refined Venetian lady Desdemona, has paid large sums of money for baubles for Iago to pass to Desdemona. Roderigo expects Iago to relay the gifts to win Desdemona's love so Roderigo can marry her. The two men learn that Desdemona has left the house of her father, Brabantio, a senator, and has eloped with Othello, a black-skinned Moor from North Africa who is a mercenary military commander in service to Venice.

Roderigo fears that he has lost both his lady and his investment. Iago reveals to Roderigo that Iago takes pleasure in plotting and lying to get what he wants. An experienced soldier, Iago hates Othello for promoting Michael Cassio, an intellectual accountant, to the position of lieutenant, a post that Iago wanted for himself. Iago plans to ruin Othello for two reasons—to avenge himself on the general for the lost promotion and to gain Desdemona for Roderigo.

Iago and Roderigo knock at the senator's door and yell until Brabantio comes out onto the upstairs balcony of his residence in his night clothes. Iago informs the senator that Desdemona has eloped with Othello. The couple room at the Sagittary Inn. Brabantio, enraged, dresses and joins Roderigo in awakening kinsmen and neighbors and in organizing a search party.

Scene 2

Iago informs Cassio of Othello's marriage. Cassio summons Othello to an urgent state meeting about the military situation on the island of Cyprus. Iago warns Othello that there may be a legal attempt to annul the marriage. Despite personal threat on his wedding day, Othello knows his military worth to Venice. He confidently meets the Duke and senators in the council chamber.

When Brabantio's party arrives at the Duke's chambers, the senator threatens Othello and accuses him of bewitching Desdemona to win her love. The angry father believes that Desdemona would never marry a black like Othello voluntarily. Brabantio calls for Othello's arrest and imprisonment, but yields to the Duke's summons to the emergency session.

Scene 3

Several reports from Cyprus in the eastern Mediterranean indicate a Turkish fleet advancing on the island. The reports differ in the size of the enemy navy, but the situation is obviously critical after the combined force heads for Rhodes, then changes course toward Cyprus. Othello enters the meeting with Cassio, Brabantio, Iago, and others. The Duke immediately appoints Othello to head the forces in defense of Cyprus.

Brabantio informs the Duke that a seducer has corrupted Desdemona with magic potions and minerals. In Brabantio's opinion, she would never willingly choose such an outsider for a husband. The Duke promises to support Brabantio's investigation of witchcraft, a capital crime. When the Duke realizes that the alleged seducer is Othello, he calls on the general to defend himself.

Othello describes his courtship of Desdemona in a dignified, persuasive speech. To prove that the romance is mutual, Othello asks the Duke to send for Desdemona to speak for herself. Iago leads a group to fetch her from the Sagittary Inn. When Othello finishes describing how he wooed Desdemona with stories of his many experiences, the Duke sides with Othello. The Duke admits that his own daughter would love a man who has survived enslavement. Desdemona makes a compelling argument concerning woman's duties. She owes obedience and gratitude to her father for her upbringing, but, after marriage, her loyalty passed to her husband, just as her mother appropriately left her father's care and passed to Brabantio's control. The Duke urges Brabantio to drop his opposition to the marriage.

Othello must depart immediately for Cyprus to command its defense. Desdemona requests to go as well. The Duke grants her wish. Before departing that night, Othello selects Iago to follow later in another ship, bringing Desdemona and her household. Iago's wife, Emilia, serves Desdemona as lady-in-waiting, a combination of chaperone, social secretary, and lady's maid. As Othello leaves, Brabantio warns Othello that Desdemona may trick her new husband just as she deceived her father. Othello trusts Desdemona's fidelity.

In private to Iago, Roderigo admits he has lost Desdemona and talks of drowning himself. Iago scorns Roderigo's melodrama and convinces him to go to Cyprus. Iago predicts that Desdemona will tire of Othello and look for younger, more interesting men. Because he hates Othello, Iago pledges to help Roderigo court Desdemona and reminds Roderigo to bring plenty of money to buy gifts to sway Desdemona into a sexual liaison.

In private, Iago congratulates himself for gaining Roderigo's money. In a side thought, Iago ponders a rumor that Othello has seduced his wife Emilia. Although Iago is unconvinced, he uses the rumor to justify his hatred. Iago's real aim is to seize Cassio's position as lieutenant, which Iago believes he deserves.

ACT II

Scene 1

On the fortified island of Cyprus, Montano, the governor, awaits the Venetian forces, whom a storm delayed at sea. A messenger reports that the Turkish fleet is so damaged by wind and waves that it no longer threatens Cyprus. Cassio's ship outruns the convoy and precedes Desdemona's ship in arriving at the harbor. Her first question is for news of Othello, whose ship the storm separated from the fleet. Cassio and Desdemona pass the time in pleasantries. Iago watches, planning to damn Cassio for his winsome courtesies to women.

Othello arrives triumphant. He, Desdemona, and their company enter the fortress. The flag bearer stays behind to fetch the general's luggage. Iago uses the opportunity to tell Roderigo a blatant lie—that Desdemona is in love with Cassio. Iago convinces Roderigo to pick a fight with Cassio to cause mutiny that will ruin Cassio's career. Iago mutters to himself his hatred for Othello, whom Iago plans to drive insane.

Scene 2

A messenger reads a proclamation declaring a night of feasting for islanders. The festivities celebrate both the destruction of the Turkish fleet and Othello and Desdemona's recent marriage.

Scene 3

During six hours of dining, merrymaking, and drinking, Cassio commands the night watch. General Othello directs the soldiers to drink with moderation and to keep the peace before the 11:00 P.M. curfew. Cassio and Iago, Othello's second in command, depart to launch a security patrol. Othello and Desdemona retire to spend their first night together since their marriage.

In private to Cassio, Iago makes suggestive remarks about Desdemona, which Cassio ignores. Iago urges Cassio to drink, despite Cassio's knowledge that he gets drunk easily. Iago spurs Roderigo into a fight with Cassio, whose military skill Roderigo belittles. When others join the melee, Iago sends Roderigo to ring the alarm bell. The noise awakens Othello, who leads an armed squad to the disturbance. The general demands to know who started the fight. Iago names Cassio. Othello relieves Cassio from his post for being drunk and disorderly while on duty. Othello and Desdemona return to bed.

Pretending friendship, Iago advises Cassio to ask Desdemona to intervene with Othello to regain Cassio's appointment. Cassio agrees. Iago uses his unsuspecting wife Emilia as a go-between to arrange a private meeting between Cassio and Desdemona.

ACT III

Scene 1

Cassio hires a group of musicians to entertain Othello. During the singing, Cassio sends a jokester to find Desdemona's lady-in-waiting. Iago dispatches Emilia from the castle to speak with Cassio. Emilia reports that Desdemona and Othello are discussing last night's street brawl. Desdemona sides with Cassio. Othello, who likes the lieutenant, promises to restore Cassio's promotion when the right moment comes.

Scene 2

Othello sends a ship-borne letter back to the Duke in Venice and begins inspecting the island fortifications.

Scene 3

Cassio asks Desdemona to intercede with Othello to restore Cassio to the rank of lieutenant. Desdemona agrees because Cassio is Othello's old friend. She promises to bring up the matter with her husband repeatedly until Othello resolves the quarrel and recalls Cassio.

When Othello and Iago enter, Cassio is embarrassed because of his drunken antics the previous night. Cassio embraces Desdemona and departs without talking to the general. Iago begins to undermine Othello's trust in his wife by interpreting Cassio's behavior as suspicious. At Desdemona's request, Othello agrees to confer with Cassio. In private to the general, Iago implies that he knows some secret evil. Othello refuses to suspect his bride of sexual infidelity.

Doubt and suspicion gnaw at Othello, who regards as faults his age and race. He agrees with Brabantio that it was unnatural for Desdemona to love him, that he was too unappealing to be loved, and that the match could not last. Iago leaves Othello, who contemplates the possibility that he married a cunning flirt who is already eyeing other men. He fears that he must wipe her out of his heart. He tries to dissuade himself from doubting Desdemona.

After Desdemona returns, Othello watches her intently for signs of betrayal. When she seeks to sooth his headache, he brushes away her handkerchief. After they go to dinner, Emilia picks up the fallen handkerchief, which Iago often urged her to steal. Emilia decides to have someone embroider a copy with strawberries to give to Iago. When he sees the handkerchief, he snatches it for his own use.

On Othello's re-entry, Iago observes the general's fevered speech. Othello believes that his wife has betrayed him and demands that Iago produce proof of Desdemona's infidelity. Iago claims that Cassio spoke in his sleep, embraced and kissed him, called him Desdemona, and cursed the general. Iago adds that he has seen Cassio wipe his forehead with a handkerchief embroidered with strawberries. Othello recognizes the handkerchief as the love token he gave to Desdemona.

Othello calls for vengeance and kneels to pledge himself to justice. Also kneeling, Iago swears to help him punish Desdemona and Cassio for their illicit affair. Iago agrees to assassinate Cassio for Othello. The general ponders how to kill Desdemona.

Scene 4

Desdemona sends for Cassio to tell him that she has spoken with Othello. She frets over the loss of her handkerchief. When Othello enters, he claims to have a head cold and rejects the cloth she uses to bind his forehead. He demands that she use the embroidered handkerchief. Desdemona tries to deflect his questions about the love token. Othello recounts the history of the handkerchief, which an Egyptian magician gave Othello's mother to keep Othello's father from straying to other women. Before the mother's death, she passed the handkerchief to Othello to give his future wife.

Desdemona contends that she has not misplaced the handkerchief. When she again brings up Cassio's demotion, Othello stomps out in fury. Desdemona mourns the loss of the love token and quails at the change in Othello's demeanor.

After Iago plants Desdemona's handkerchief in Cassio's lodgings, Cassio discovers it and gives it to his mistress Bianca. Cassio asks her to make a copy of it to keep after he returns the original to its owner. Bianca immediately suspects that it belongs to a woman. She berates Cassio for being apart from her for seven days and accuses him of having another mistress.

ACT IV

Scene 1

To Othello, Iago lies that Cassio has confessed to sexual dalliance with Desdemona. The general faints from rage. When Cassio enters, Iago claims that Othello has had seizures before. Rather than revive him, Iago instructs Cassio to let the fit wear off naturally and to come back later. Othello, regaining consciousness, berates himself as a husband tricked by an unchaste wife. Iago tells him to hide and observe Cassio when he returns. Iago says he will urge Cassio to relate his amorous adventures with Desdemona.

Othello withdraws in turmoil from Iago's manipulations. Iago talks with Cassio about Bianca. From a distance, Othello sees Cassio smile and laugh at the thought of marrying a street walker like Bianca. Othello believes that Cassio is joking about how much Desdemona loves him. Bianca enters bearing Desdemona's handkerchief, which she throws at Cassio. Seeing Bianca disrespect his wife's handkerchief, Othello believes that Desdemona is unfaithful. He plans to restore justice by killing both Cassio and Desdemona that very night.

Lodovico appears with news that the Duke has recalled Othello to Venice and has placed Cassio in the governorship. Because Desdemona approves the assignments, Othello slaps his wife. Lodovico is amazed at the crude behavior of a man who is usually restrained. Iago hints that Othello often acts violently.

Scene 2

When Othello questions Emilia, she assures him that nothing immodest has taken place between her mistress and Cassio. Othello believes Desdemona has managed to deceive even her lady-in-waiting. Speaking with his wife in private, Othello threatens to banish her. He calls her "whore" and "strumpet," charges that confuse and upset her. She immediately denies wrongdoing.

When Othello leaves, Desdemona acknowledges that he is punishing her. She ponders the cause of his rage. Emilia suspects that some villain has turned Othello against his wife and has stirred up his jealousy with gossip and lies. When Desdemona asks Iago's advice, he replies that only the business of state angers Othello.

Roderigo confesses to Iago that the quest for Desdemona is hopeless. Iago urges Roderigo to kill Cassio. Iago reasons that Cassio's death will prevent Othello returning to Venice and, therefore, will keep Desdemona in Cyprus. Roderigo hesitantly agrees to the assassination plot.

Scene 3

After a state dinner, Othello orders Desdemona to go to bed and to dismiss her attendant. Desdemona and Emilia discuss the unsettling turn of events. Emilia views the marriage as a mistake, but Desdemona regrets nothing. She has a premonition of death and requests Emilia to wrap her body in one of the couple's wedding sheets, which Emilia spread on the bed. Desdemona sings the "Willow Song," which the maid Barbary sang after her lover went mad and abandoned her.

ACT V

Scene 1

In the street at night, Iago directs Roderigo to hide behind a wall and ambush Cassio. When Cassio approaches, Roderigo attacks unsuccessfully and suffers a fatal stab from Cassio's sword. Iago, from behind, stabs Cassio in the leg and runs away while Cassio cries murder. Pretending outrage, Iago organizes medical help for Cassio and arrests Bianca on suspicion of joining the ambush.

Othello, hearing Cassio's cry, believes that Iago has assassinated Desdemona's lover as planned. Following Iago's lead, Othello hardens his heart against his wife's beauty. He intends to smother her in the bed where she has betrayed him.

Scene 2

Desdemona lies asleep in bed when Othello enters. She wakens and calls to him. He orders her to pray at once, repenting her sins. He will wait while she confesses her wrongdoings because he does not want to prevent her soul from entering heaven. Desdemona realizes that Othello intends to murder her. She is afraid, but guiltless. Knowing that she cannot convince him of her fidelity, she weeps and begs him to banish her rather than kill her. She asks him to let her live a half hour, but he smothers her immediately.

When Emilia knocks, Othello shuts the bed-curtains and opens the door to hear the news. Emilia reports that Cassio has killed Roderigo. Desdemona revives, claiming to be wrongfully slain. Emilia calls for help. Desdemona says that she is innocent. Before she dies, she blames herself for her own murder.

Emilia confronts Othello and vows to risk her life to report his crime. Othello declares that he has killed Desdemona because of her infidelity.

Emilia insists that Desdemona was faithful. Othello replies that, according to Iago, Cassio defiled Desdemona. Emilia absorbs Iago's evil while Othello pours out his heart. Emilia curses Iago, calls him a liar, and cries murder to waken the castle.

Montano, Gratiano, Iago, and others rush into the bedchamber. Emilia challenges Iago to defend himself. Iago repeats his lie that Desdemona carried on an affair with Cassio. Emilia reveals how she found the handkerchief and gave it to her husband, who had asked her to steal. After ordering Emilia to be silent and to return home, Iago stabs her and runs out. As she dies, Emilia tells Othello that Desdemona loved him. Othello realizes that Iago has tricked and manipulated him into murdering his bride.

The guard apprehends Iago. Othello and Cassio demand to know why Iago plotted so unthinkable a crime. Iago refuses to explain and says he will never speak again. Othello, watching his world unravel, asks the men to remember him clearly, his good points and his bad. After admitting that he loved Desdemona too much rather than too little, he stabs himself, falls on the bed next to her, and dies.

Lodovico takes charge, giving Othello's house and property to Gratiano, the general's next of kin by marriage. Cassio takes command of Cyprus and receives Lodovico's order to torture Iago. Lodovico will return to Venice with news of multiple violent deaths.

List of Characters

OTHELLO   A Moor (a North African), a general in the defense forces of the city-state of Venice. His successful profession brings him high status in Venice, but his foreign origins and color separate him from those with whom he lives and works. He is a military man, with a reputation for courage in battle and good judgment in military matters. Othello falls in love and marries Desdemona, but during the campaign against the Turks, Iago tricks Othello into believing that his wife has been unfaithful with his lieutenant, Cassio. Iago works on Othello's personal and social insecurity until Othello believes the combination of Iago's lies and flimsy circumstantial evidence. Inflamed with jealousy, he smothers Desdemona in her bed, only to find out too late that he has been misled and has killed the woman who loved him faithfully. In despair, he stabs himself to death.

IAGO   Othello's *ancient* (flag bearer) in the Venetian defense forces. He had hoped for promotion, but Othello passed over him in favor of Cassio. Iago works revenge on them both. He exploits Roderigo as a source of money and an unwitting accomplice in his plot to bring down Othello. When finally cornered and charged with his wickedness, Iago refuses to speak or to repent or explain his actions. Lodovico puts Cassio in charge of Iago's torture.

DESDEMONA   A noble Venetian lady, daughter of the widower Brabantio. She organizes her life intelligently and shows courage, love, and loyalty in following her husband into danger. She accompanies Othello to Cyprus on the campaign against the Turks. To her surprise, he turns sour and spiteful, accuses her of adultery, and slaps her in public. She clings to an innocent love of her husband. When she realizes he is about to kill her, she can feel only despair and grief. She dies declaring her love for him.

BRABANTIO   A Venetian senator, Desdemona's father. He is outraged at his daughter's elopement with a Moorish general. He demands Othello's imprisonment for bewitching Desdemona. He can do nothing once the marriage has taken place, and the Venetian Senate has accepted it. He warns Othello that Desdemona is a clever deceiver. Brabantio dies of grief.

RODERIGO   A Venetian nobleman in love with Desdemona. He has more money than sense and pays Iago to court Desdemona on his behalf. Iago, playing on Roderigo's hopes and gullibility, continues to help himself to Roderigo's money. Roderigo never gets his heart's desire. To ensure his silence, Iago involves Roderigo in an attack on Cassio, for which Roderigo pays with his life, after Iago stabs him.

CASSIO   Othello's lieutenant in the Venetian defense forces. Cassio accompanied Othello as his friend when he was courting Desdemona. Cassio is popular, well-spoken, lively, and trusting but easily inebriated by wine. Iago eventually convinces Othello that Cassio is Desdemona's paramour. Appointed governor of Cyprus after Othello's death, Cassio superintends Iago's torture.

BIANCA   A courtesan (prostitute), in love with Cassio. She is skilled in needlework and agrees to copy the handkerchief that Cassio gives her. She throws it back at him, believing it is the token of his new love.

EMILIA   Desdemona's lady-in-waiting and Iago's wife. She knows Iago better than anybody and suspects his actions and motives. She does not realize until too late that the wicked person who has poisoned Othello against Desdemona is Iago, her own husband.

THE DUKE OF VENICE   The leader of the governing body of the city-state of Venice. The Duke appoints Othello to lead the forces defending Venice against the Turkish attack on Cyprus. In the uproar over Othello's elopement with Desdemona, a senator's daughter, the Duke urges Brabantio to accept the marriage.

GRATIANO   Desdemona's uncle. He and Lodovico find Cassio wounded after Roderigo stabs him in the drunken brawl. Gratiano reports Brabantio's death from grief. As the only family survivor, Gratiano inherits Othello's property.

LODOVICO   A Venetian ambassador. He witnesses Othello slapping Desdemona. After her murder, Lodovico takes charge and gives Othello's property to Gratiano. The ambassador questions Othello and Cassio together, thus revealing the truth.

MONTANO   Othello's predecessor as the governor of Cyprus. He is Othello's friend and loyal supporter. Cassio wounds the ex-governor in a street brawl.

Character Map

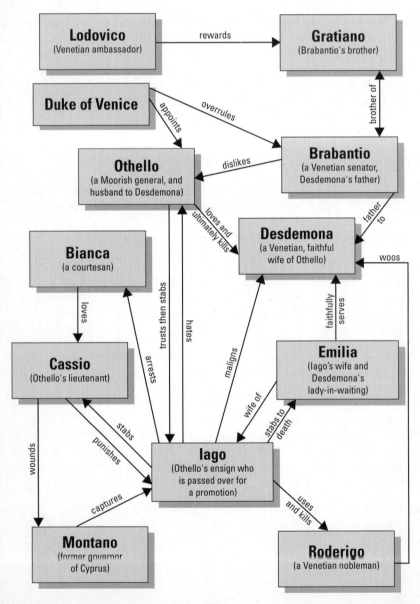

Cycle of Death

In a vicious cycle of assaults and murder derived from the jealousy of one man, Iago, the graphic below outlines the sequence of the deaths that advance the tragic plot.

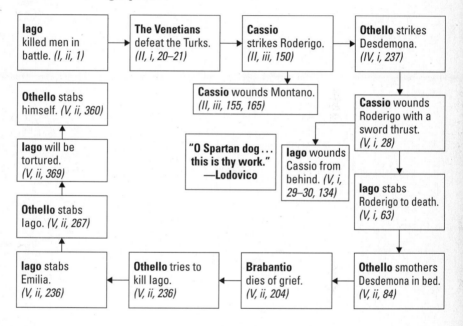

| **Iago** killed men in battle. *(I, ii, 1)* | **The Venetians** defeat the Turks. *(II, i, 20–21)* | **Cassio** strikes Roderigo. *(II, iii, 150)* | **Othello** strikes Desdemona. *(IV, i, 237)* |

Cassio wounds Montano. *(II, iii, 155, 165)*

Othello stabs himself. *(V, ii, 360)*

Cassio wounds Roderigo with a sword thrust. *(V, i, 28)*

Iago will be tortured. *(V, ii, 369)*

"O Spartan dog . . . this is thy work."
—Lodovico

Iago wounds Cassio from behind. *(V, i, 29–30, 134)*

Othello stabs Iago. *(V, ii, 267)*

Iago stabs Roderigo to death. *(V, i, 63)*

| **Iago** stabs Emilia. *(V, ii, 236)* | **Othello** tries to kill Iago. *(V, ii, 236)* | **Brabantio** dies of grief. *(V, ii, 204)* | **Othello** smothers Desdemona in bed. *(V, ii, 84)* |

Shakespeare's
Othello

ACT I, SCENE 1

A street in Venice. Night.

[Enter RODERIGO and IAGO]

RODERIGO   Tush, never tell me! I take it much unkindly
That thou, Iago, who hast had my purse
As if the strings were thine, should'st know of this.

IAGO   'Sblood, but you will not hear me!
If ever I did dream of such a matter,   5
Abhor me.

RODERIGO   Thou told'st me thou didst hold him in thy hate.

IAGO   Despise me if I do not. Three great ones of the city,
In personal suit to make me his lieutenant,
Off-capped to him; and, by the faith of man,   10
I know my price; I am worth no worse a place.
But he, as loving his own pride and purposes,
Evades them with a bombast circumstance.
Horribly stuffed with epithets of war;
And, in conclusion,   15
Nonsuits my mediators; for, 'Certes,' says he,
'I have already chose my officer.'
And what was he?
Forsooth, a great arithmetician,
One Michael Cassio, a Florentine   20
(A fellow almost damned in a fair wife)
That never set a squadron in the field,
Nor the division of a battle knows
More than a spinster; unless the bookish theoric,
Wherein the togèd consuls can propose   25
As masterly as he. Mere prattle without practice
Is all his soldiership. But he, sir, had th' election;
And I (of whom his eyes had seen the proof
At Rhodes, at Cyprus, and on other grounds
Christian and heathen) must be belee'd and calmed   30
By debitor and creditor; this counter-caster,
He, in good time, must his lieutenant be,
And I—God bless the mark!—his Moorship's ancient.

RODERIGO   By heaven, I rather would have been his hangman.

ACT I, SCENE 1

A street in Venice, a city-state in eastern Italy, at night.

[RODERIGO and IAGO enter.]

RODERIGO   Hush, don't say it! I am insulted that you, Iago, who has held my wallet as if it were yours, should know of this scandal.

IAGO   God's blood, why won't you listen! If I only imagined it, you can hate me for telling you a fantasy.

RODERIGO   You told me you hate Othello.

IAGO   You can loathe me if I lied about hating Othello. Three city dignitaries carried hats in hand to plead for my pro-motion to lieutenant, an honor that Cassio won. By human standards, I know my worth. I deserve no lower a position. But Othello, wrapped up in pride and ambition, tricks them with high-sounding speeches filled with boasts of battlefield deeds. In the end, my promoters lost their case because, in Othello's words, "I am sure of the man I want for my second-in-command." And who is the winner of the office—a smart tactician, Michael Cassio, from Florence, a city-state in western Italy. (A man ruined by chasing a pretty woman.) Cassio has no battlefield experience and knows no more about plotting battlelines than an old maid. All he knows are abstract battles writ-ten on a page, a skill that peaceloving statesmen can master as well as Cassio. All Cassio knows about soldiery is only talk, not action. But, Roderigo, the statesmen voted for Cassio instead of me. And I, who have fought wars on the Mediterranean islands of Rhodes and Cyprus and in Christian and alien places, must remain behind and take a non-combat role second to this bookkeeper. This accountant will shortly assume the post of lieu-tenant. And I—damn the title!—become the black man's flag bearer.

RODERIGO   Heaven knows, I would rather be the black man's executioner.

TRANSLATION

IAGO	Why, there's no remedy; 'tis the curse of service.	35
	Preferment goes by letter and affection,	
	And not by old gradation, where each second	
	Stood heir to th' first. Now, sir, be judge yourself,	
	Whether I in any just term am affined	
	To love the Moor.	40

RODERIGO   I would not follow him then.

IAGO	O, sir, content you;	
	I follow him to serve my turn upon him.	
	We cannot all be masters, nor all masters	
	Cannot be truly followed. You shall mark	
	Many a duteous and knee-crooking knave	45
	That, doting on his own obsequious bondage,	
	Wears out his time, much like his master's ass,	
	For naught but provender; and when he's old, cashiered.	
	Whip me such honest knaves! Others there are	
	Who, trimmed in forms and visages of duty,	50
	Keep yet their hearts attending on themselves;	
	And, throwing but shows of service on their lords,	
	Do well thrive by them, and when they have lined their coats,	
	Do themselves homage. These fellows have some soul;	
	And such a one do I profess myself. For, sir,	55
	It is as sure as you are Roderigo,	
	Were I the Moor, I would not be Iago.	
	In following him, I follow but myself;	
	Heaven is my judge, not I for love and duty,	
	But seeming so, for my peculiar end;	60
	For when my outward action doth demonstrate	
	The native act and figure of my heart	
	In compliment extern, 'tis not long after	
	But I will wear my heart upon my sleeve	
	For daws to peck at; I am not what I am.	65

RODERIGO	What a full fortune does the thick-lips owe
	If he can carry't thus!

IAGO	Call up her father,	
	Rouse him. Make after him, poison his delight,	
	Proclaim him in the streets. Incense her kinsmen,	
	And though he in a fertile climate dwell,	70
	Plague him with flies; though that his joy be joy,	
	Yet throw such changes of vexation on't	
	As it may lose some color.	

RODERIGO   Here is her father's house. I'll call aloud

IAGO

There's no way to change matters; unfair promotions are a military curse. Soldiers advance through influence and by making friends with superiors, not by seniority, where the second-in-command eventually replaces the commander-in-chief. Now, Roderigo, you tell me if I have to like the black man.

RODERIGO

If it were me, I would not serve in his army.

IAGO

Just wait; I will serve under him until I can pay him back for his unfair choice. Some people aren't meant to be leaders deserving a loyal following. You have noticed how many obedient and fawning slackers, pretending to serve him humbly, waste their term of service, just like the leader's donkey, and receive only daily upkeep. When the donkey is too old to serve, he's tossed out of the army. In my opinion, such noble bootlickers should be whipped! There are other soldiers who, making a show of a spruce appearance and soldierly duty, conceal their self-interest. While pretending to be loyal to their superior officers, these rogues better themselves with unearned admiration and praise. These self-seekers have spirit. I claim to be just like them. As certainly as you are Roderigo, if I were the black man, I would not be the cast-off Iago. In carrying his flag, I benefit only myself; let God judge me, that I pretend to honor and serve the black man, but I do so only for my own gain. By the time that my outward behavior displays my real self, I will make myself vulnerable to criticism. I am not showing the world the real me.

RODERIGO

The black man will be lucky to get away with promoting Cassio.

IAGO

Call Desdemona's father, wake him up. Harass Brabantio, ruin his joy, yell his name from the streets. Outrage her relatives, and though Brabantio lives comfortably, irritate him with petty annoyances. Though the father is really joyous, shift his view of this situation from glad to doubtful.

RODERIGO

Here is Brabantio's house. I'll yell for him.

IAGO	Do, with like timorous accent and dire yell	75
	As when, by night and negligence, the fire	
	Is spied in populous cities.	

RODERIGO   What, ho, Brabantio! Signior Brabantio, ho!

IAGO   Awake! What, ho, Brabantio! Thieves! thieves! thieves!
Look to your house, your daughter, and your bags!   80
Thieves! thieves!
[BRABANTIO at a window]

BRABANTIO   *[Above]* What is the reason of this terrible summons?
What is the matter there?

RODERIGO   Signior, is all your family within?

IAGO   Are your doors locked?   85

BRABANTIO   Why, wherefore ask you this?

IAGO   Zounds, sir, y'are robbed! For shame, put on your gown!
Your heart is burst; you have lost half your soul.
Even now, now, very now, an old black ram
Is tupping your white ewe. Arise, arise!
Awake the snorting citizens with the bell,   90
Or else the devil will make a grandsire of you.
Arise, I say!

BRABANTIO   What, have you lost your wits?

RODERIGO   Most reverend signior, do you know my voice?

BRABANTIO   Not I. What are you?

RODERIGO   My name is Roderigo.   95

BRABANTIO   The worser welcome!
I have charged thee not to haunt about my doors.
In honest plainness thou hast heard me say
My daughter is not for thee; and now, in madness,
Being full of supper and distemp'ring draughts,
Upon malicious bravery dost thou come   100
To start my quiet.

RODERIGO   Sir, sir, sir—

BRABANTIO   But thou must needs be sure
My spirit and my place have in them power
To make this bitter to thee.

RODERIGO   Patience, good sir.

IAGO	Yes, raise a noise like the alert to an emergency, such as a fire in a big city flaring up during the night from carelessness.
RODERIGO	Brabantio! Are you there? Brabantio, sir, hello!
IAGO	Get up! Brabantio, are you there! Robbers! Check your home, your wallet, and your daughter! Vandals! *[BRABANTIO comes to an upper-story window.]*
BRABANTIO	*[Looking down]* What is the reason for this uproar? What is the problem?
RODERIGO	Sir, is all your family home?
IAGO	Are your doors still locked?
BRABANTIO	Why do you ask?
IAGO	God's wounds, sir, you've been robbed! Put on your robe! Someone has broken your heart and stolen half your soul. At this very moment, an old black man is stealing your white daughter's virginity. Get up, get up! Ring the city alarm bell before the black man impregnates your daughter. Get up, quickly!
BRABANTIO	Are you out of your mind?
RODERIGO	Honored sir, do you recognize my voice?
BRABANTIO	No. Who are you?
RODERIGO	I am Roderigo.
BRABANTIO	Someone worse than you would be more welcome. I have ordered you away from my door. I have told you plainly that you can't marry my daughter. Now, like a madman, you have left your dinner and too much to drink and come out of foolish darings to annoy my sleep.
RODERIGO	Please, sir.
BRABANTIO	Don't forget that I have the guts and power to make you regret this disturbance.
RODERIGO	Please wait, sir.

BRABANTIO	What tell'st thou me of robbing? This is Venice; 105 My house is not a grange.
RODERIGO	Most grave Brabantio, In simple and pure soul I come to you.
IAGO	Zounds, sir, you are one of those that will not serve God if the devil bid you. Because we come to do you service, and you think we are ruffians, you'll 110 have your daughter covered by a Barbary horse; you'll have your nephews neigh to you; you'll have coursers for cousins, and gennets for germans.
BRABANTIO	What profane wretch art thou?
IAGO	I am one, sir, that comes to tell you your 115 daughter and the Moor are now making the beast with two backs.
BRABANTIO	Thou art a villain.
IAGO	You are—a senator.
BRABANTIO	This thou shalt answer. I know thee, Roderigo.
RODERIGO	Sir, I will answer anything. But I beseech you, 120 If't be your pleasure and most wise consent, As partly I find it is, that your fair daughter, At this odd-even and dull watch o' th' night, Transported, with no worse nor better guard But with a knave of common hire, a gondolier, 125 To the gross clasps of a lascivious Moor— If this be known to you, and your allowance, We then have done you bold and saucy wrongs; But if you know not this, my manners tell me We have your wrong rebuke. Do not believe 130 That, from the sense of all civility, I thus would play and trifle with your reverence. Your daughter, if you have not given her leave, I say again, hath made a gross revolt, Tying her duty, beauty, wit, and fortunes 135 In an extravagant and wheeling stranger Of here and everywhere. Straight satisfy yourself. If she be in her chamber, or your house, Let loose on me the justice of the state For thus deluding you. 140

ORIGINAL

BRABANTIO   What are you yelling about thieves? This is the city of Venice; I don't live out in the backcountry.

RODERIGO   Noble Brabantio, I come with simple, honest truth.

IAGO   God's wounds, sir, you are misjudging the messengers. Because you waste time charging us with being villains, you are allowing a barbarian stallion to dishonor your daughter. Your nephews will be colts; your cousins will be race horses; and your closest relatives will be part-Spanish.

BRABANTIO   What rude-mouthed vulgarian is this?

IAGO   I am the person who comes to inform you that the black man is making love to your daughter.

BRABANTIO   You are crude.

IAGO   You are an esteemed senator.

BRABANTIO   You will pay for this. I recognize you, Roderigo.

RODERIGO   Sir, I will face my punishment, but I beg you. If you are content that your daughter in the dead of night has eloped, with no more security guard than a hired gondolier, to the embrace of a lustful black man, if you agree to their relationship, then we have rudely insulted you. But if you don't know of this elopement, then you have unfairly scolded us. Don't think that I, a courteous man, would make fun of your dignity. Your daughter, if you have not betrothed her to the black man, has slipped away and pledged her honor, beauty, sense, and inheritance to a dashing, gallivanting stranger. Check for yourself. If she is in her room or in the residence, charge me with wrongdoing for tricking you.

TRANSLATION

BRABANTIO   Strike on the tinder, ho!
Give me a taper! Call up all my people!
This accident is not unlike my dream.
Belief of it oppresses me already.
Light, I say! light! *[Exit above]*

IAGO   Farewell, for I must leave you.
It seems not meet, nor wholesome to my place,   145
To be produced—as, if I stay, I shall—
Against the Moor. For I do know the state,
However this may gall him with some check,
Cannot with safety cast him; for he's embarked
With such loud reason to the Cyprus wars,   150
Which even now stand in act, that for their souls
Another of his fathom they have none
To lead their business; in which regard,
Though I do hate him as I do hell-pains,
Yet, for necessity of present life,   155
I must show out a flag and sign of love,
Which is indeed but sign. That you shall surely find him,
Lead to the Sagittary the raised search;
And there will I be with him. So farewell. *[Exit]*
*[Enter, below, BRABANTIO in his nightgown, and Servants
with torches]*

BRABANTIO   It is too true an evil. Gone she is;   160
And what's to come of my despised time
Is naught but bitterness. Now Roderigo,
Where didst thou see her?—O unhappy girl!—
With the Moor, say'st thou?—Who would be a father?—
How didst thou know 'twas she?—O, she deceives me   165
Past thought!—What said she to you?—Get moe tapers!
Raise all my kindred!—Are they married, think you?

RODERIGO   Truly I think they are.

BRABANTIO   O heaven! How got she out? O treason of the blood!
Fathers, from hence trust not your daughters' minds   170
But what you see them act. Is there not charms
By which the property of youth and maidhood
May be abused? Have you not read, Roderigo,
Of some such thing?

RODERIGO   Yes, sir, I have indeed.

BRABANTIO   Call up my brother.—O, would you had had her!— 175
Some one way, some another.—Do you know
Where we may apprehend her and the Moor?

ORIGINAL

BRABANTIO	Strike a light, there! Hand me a candle. Wake up the household! I'm already afraid the elopement really did happen. A candle, I command you, a candle! *[BRABANTIO departs from the upstairs window.]*
IAGO	Goodbye; I have to go. It isn't proper nor in keeping with my military position to testify against Othello if I stay here. I know the political situation. Even if I have embarrassed Othello, the charge is not strong enough to ruin him. The black man has made so good a case for a war against Cyprus that, while the army stands ready to attack, there is no other commander to take Othello's place. Even though I despise the black man like condemnation to hell, for the time being, I have to bear his flag and pretend to honor him with an outward show of duty. To locate Othello, search the Archer Inn, where I will join him. Goodbye. *[IAGO goes out.]* *[BRABANTIO, dressed in his night clothes, enters from the first floor along with servants carrying torches.]*
BRABANTIO	What a terrible wrong. My daughter is gone. The rest of my life will be miserable. Roderigo, where did you see her? Oh, wretched girl! She went with Othello, you say? Who would want to have children? How did you recognize her? Oh, she is trickier than I thought possible. What did she tell you? Give me more candles! Awaken my relatives! Did Desdemona marry Othello?
RODERIGO	I think they are already wed.
BRABANTIO	Oh, God! How did she escape? Betrayal by my own daughter! Parents, don't trust anything from your daughters but what you see them doing. Aren't there love potions by which men charm young girls and steal their virginity? Have you read of such drugs, Roderigo?
RODERIGO	Yes, sir, I certainly have.
BRABANTIO	Summon my brother. Oh, I wish you had married my daughter! Some of you go this way, some that way. Do you know where I can find my daughter and Othello?

RODERIGO   I think I can discover him, if you please
           To get good guard and go along with me.

BRABANTIO Pray you lead on. At every house I'll call: 180
           I may command at most.—Get weapons, ho!
           And raise some special officers of night.—
           On, good Roderigo; I'll deserve your pains.
           [Exeunt]

RODERIGO   I think I can locate him. Please order security guards and follow me.

BRABANTIO   Go ahead. I will stop at every house. Most will respect my prestigious position. Arm yourselves! Call the night watch. Go on, Roderigo; I will pay you for your service. *[They go out.]*

ACT I, SCENE 2

Another street.

[Enter OTHELLO, IAGO, and Attendants with torches]

IAGO   Though in the trade of war I have slain men,
        Yet do I hold it very stuff o' th' conscience
        To do no contrived murther. I lack iniquity
        Sometimes to do me service. Nine or ten times
        I had thought t' have yerked him here under the ribs.   5

OTHELLO   'Tis better as it is.

IAGO   Nay, but he prated,
        And spoke such scurvy and provoking terms
        Against your honor
        That with the little godliness I have
        I did full hard forbear him. But I pray you, sir,   10
        Are you fast married? Be assured of this,
        That the magnifico is much beloved,
        And hath in his effect a voice potential
        As double as the Duke's. He will divorce you,
        Or put upon you what restraint and grievance   15
        The law, with all his might to enforce it on,
        Will give him cable.

OTHELLO   Let him do his spite.
        My services which I have done the signiory
        Shall out-tongue his complaints. 'Tis yet to know—
        Which, when I know that boasting is an honor,   20
        I shall promulgate—I fetch my life and being
        From men of royal siege; and my demerits
        May speak unbonneted to as proud a fortune
        As this that I have reached. For know, Iago,
        But that I love the gentle Desdemona,   25
        I would not my unhoused free condition
        Put into circumscription and confine
        For the sea's worth.
        [Enter CASSIO, with torches, Officers]
                            But look, what lights come yond?

IAGO   Those are the raised father and his friends.
        You were best go in.   30

ACT I, SCENE 2

On another street in Venice.

[OTHELLO, IAGO, and torch-bearers enter.]

IAGO   Although I have killed men in battle, I think murder is immoral. I am not evil enough to kill a man. Nine or ten times I have imagined stabbing Brabantio in the gut.

OTHELLO   I am glad you didn't murder him.

IAGO   But he gossiped and spread such scandal against you that I could hardly follow my conscience and tolerate him. Please, Othello, are you already married? Be warned that Brabantio is generally admired and has the potential of twice the Duke's power. Brabantio will separate you from his daughter or press charges as far as the law and his influence allow.

OTHELLO   Let him do what he wants. My performance on behalf of Venice shall outweigh his petty grievances. Venetians don't yet know of my accomplishments. I shall announce them along with my royal ancestry only when it is honorable to brag. And my honors shall speak plain that I deserve my current position. I tell you, Iago, even though I love Desdemona, I would not give up my personal liberty for all the treasure in the ocean. *[CASSIO and the night watch enter with torches.]* Look ahead, who is coming this way with torches?

IAGO   Those are the torches of Brabantio and his supporters. You must get out of the street.

TRANSLATION

OTHELLO	Not I; I must be found.
	My parts, my title, and my perfect soul
	Shall manifest me rightly. It is they?
IAGO	By Janus, I think no.
OTHELLO	The servants of the Duke, and my lieutenant.
	The goodness of the night upon you, friends! 35
	What is the news?
CASSIO	The Duke does greet you general;
	And he requires your haste-post-haste appearance
	Even on the instant.
OTHELLO	What's the matter, think you?
CASSIO	Something from Cyprus, as I may divine.
	It is a business of some heat. The galleys 40
	Have sent a dozen sequent messengers
	This very night at one another's heels,
	And many of the consuls, raised and met,
	Are at the Duke's already. You have been hotly called for;
	When, being not at your lodging to be found, 45
	The Senate hath sent about three several quests
	To search you out.
OTHELLO	'Tis well I am found by you.
	I will but spend a word here in the house,
	And go with you. *[Exit]*
CASSIO	Ancient, what makes he here?
IAGO	Faith, he to-night hath boarded a land carack 50
	If it prove lawful prize, he's made for ever.
CASSIO	I do not understand.
IAGO	He's married.
CASSIO	To who?
	[Enter OTHELLO]
IAGO	Marry, to—Come, captain, will you go?
OTHELLO	Have with you.
CASSIO	Here comes another troop to seek for you.
	[Enter BRABANTIO, RODERIGO, and others with lights and weapons]
IAGO	It is Brabantio. General, be advised. 55
	He comes to bad intent.

ORIGINAL

OTHELLO	Not me. I intend to face them. My worth, my rank, and my clean conscience will put me in the right. Is it Brabantio's party?
IAGO	By the two-faced god Janus, I don't think so.
OTHELLO	It is the Duke's men and my lieutenant Cassio. A good evening to you, friends! What is happening?
CASSIO	The Duke sends his greetings, General Othello, and needs to see you as soon as possible.
OTHELLO	What is the reason, in your opinion?
CASSIO	A message from the island of Cyprus, as I understand it. It is serious business. The warships have sent twelve messengers one after another tonight and awakened counselors, who have gathered at the Duke's office. You are in great demand. When you could not be found at home, the Senate sent three different search parties to find you.
OTHELLO	I am glad you found me, Cassio. I will leave a word at this house and accompany you to the Duke's office. *[OTHELLO goes out.]*
CASSIO	Iago the flag-bearer, why does Othello stop here?
IAGO	Indeed, he has married a rich bride tonight. If the marriage is legal, he has made his fortune.
CASSIO	I don't understand.
IAGO	He's married.
CASSIO	To whom? *[OTHELLO returns.]*
IAGO	Indeed, to—Captain Cassio, I will tell you later. Will you follow Othello?
OTHELLO	Let's go to the Duke.
CASSIO	Here comes another group looking for you, Othello. *[BRABANTIO, RODERIGO, and other people arrive carrying torches and weapons.]*
IAGO	It's Brabantio. General Othello, be careful. Brabantio intends you harm.

TRANSLATION

OTHELLO   Holla! stand there!

RODERIGO   Signior, it is the Moor.

BRABANTIO   Down with him, thief!
[They draw on both sides]

IAGO   You, Roderigo! Come, sir, I am for you.

OTHELLO   Keep up your bright swords, for the dew will rust them.
                      Good signior, you shall more command with years   60
                      Than with your weapons.

BRABANTIO   O thou foul thief, where has thou stowed my daughter?
                      Damned as thou art, thou hast enchanted her!
                      For I'll refer me to all things of sense,
                      If she in chains of magic were not bound,   65
                      Whether a maid so tender, fair, and happy,
                      So opposite to marriage that she shunned
                      The wealthy curled darlings of our nation,
                      Would ever have, t' incur a general mock,
                      Run from her guardage to the sooty bosom   70
                      Of such a thing as thou—to fear, not to delight.
                      Judge me the world if 'tis not gross in sense
                      That thou hast practiced on her with foul charms,
                      Abused her delicate youth with drugs or minerals
                      That weaken motion. I'll have't disputed on;   75
                      'Tis probable, and palpable to thinking.
                      I therefore apprehend and do attach thee
                      For an abuser of the world, a practicer
                      Of arts inhibited and out of warrant.
                      Lay hold upon him. If he do resist,   80
                      Subdue him at his peril.

OTHELLO   Hold your hands,
                      Both you of my inclining and the rest.
                      Were it my cue to fight, I should have known it
                      Without a prompter. Where will you that I go
                      To answer this your charge?   85

BRABANTIO   To prison, till fit time
                      Of law and course of direct session
                      Call thee to answer.

OTHELLO	You! Halt!
RODERIGO	Sir, it is the black man.
BRABANTIO	Attack the thief! *[Both parties draw their weapons.]*
IAGO	Roderigo, face me. You are my enemy.
OTHELLO	Put up your sharpened blades, for they will rust from night moisture. Noble Brabantio, I honor your age and experience more than I fear your swords.
BRABANTIO	You wretched felon, where are you hiding my daughter? Damned demon, you have tricked her! It seems reasonable that, if you hadn't bewitched her, so naive, pretty, and contented a girl so unwilling to marry that she rejected rich, pampered young Venetians would never risk ridicule by eloping with a black. She would be more afraid than delighted to marry the likes of you. Let the world see how obvious it is that you deceived her and spoiled her young womanhood with concoctions or powders that dull the senses. I'll take it to court. My charge is likely and reasonable. I arrest and hold you as a heathen seducer, a practicer of evil, unlawful plots. Grab him. If he fights back, threaten him with death.
OTHELLO	Stop the violence, both my men and the others. If I were about to be seized, I would know how to fight back. Where will you take me to face this charge of tricking and capturing your daughter?
BRABANTIO	To the prison. You will remain there until a judge calls you to testify before the court.

OTHELLO   What if I do obey?
How may the Duke therewith satisfied,
Whose messengers are here about my side
Upon some present business of the state   90
To bring me to him?

OFFICER   'Tis true, most worthy signior.
The Duke's in council, and your noble self
I am sure is sent for.

BRABANTIO   How? The Duke in council?
In this time of the night? Bring him away.
Mine's not an idle cause. The Duke himself,   95
Or any of my brothers of the state,
Cannot but feel this wrong as 'twere their own;
For if such actions may have passage free,
Bondslaves and pagans shall our statesmen be.
[Exeunt]

ORIGINAL

OTHELLO   What will happen if I agree to go to prison? How can I serve the Duke, who has sent men to fetch me on some important state matter?

OFFICER   He is telling the truth, noble Brabantio. The Duke is holding a war council and expects you to attend.

BRABANTIO   What? The Duke has called a meeting? At this late hour? Bring Othello along. I have a serious matter to prosecute. Even the Duke or any of my fellow dignitaries can't overlook Othello's crime as though he had stolen their own daughters. If such a villain goes free, then Venice may as well be ruled by slaves and heathens. *[They go out.]*

TRANSLATION

ACT I, SCENE 3

A council chamber.

[Enter DUKE and Senators, sitting at a table, with lights and Attendants]

DUKE   There is no composition in these news
That gives them credit.

1. SENATOR   Indeed they are disproportioned.
My letters say a hundred and seven galleys.

DUKE   And mine a hundred forty.

2. SENATOR   And mine two hundred.
But though they jump not on a just account—   5
As in these cases where the aim reports
'Tis oft with difference—yet do they all confirm
A Turkish fleet, and bearing up to Cyprus.

DUKE   Nay, it is possible enough to judgment.
I do not so secure me in the error   10
But the main article I do approve
In fearful sense.

SAILOR   *[Within]* What, ho! what, ho! what ho!

OFFICER   A messenger from the galleys.
[Enter Sailor]

DUKE   Now, what's the business?

SAILOR   The Turkish preparation makes for Rhodes.
So was I bid report here to the state   15
By Signior Angelo.

DUKE   How say you by this change?

ORIGINAL

ACT I, SCENE 3

A Venetian council hall.

[The DUKE enters to sit at the table with senators and their servants, who carry candles.]

DUKE   These reports from the fleet are inconsistent.

1. SENATOR   I agree they are contradictory. My reports say 107 warships.

DUKE   My report says 140 warships.

2. SENATOR   My reports state 200 warships. Even though the reports are contradictory, they declare that a fleet of Turkish ships is sailing toward Cyprus.

DUKE   I won't quibble over details. Even though the reports differ, the Turkish intent is fearful.

SAILOR   *[Inside the building.]* What is it? What do you want?

OFFICER   I have a messenger from the warships. *[A sailor enters.]*

DUKE   What's happening now?

SAILOR   The Turks are heading for the island of Rhodes. Sir Angelo sent me here to report the advance to you.

DUKE   What do you make of this change of direction?

TRANSLATION

1. SENATOR	This cannot be
	By no assay of reason. 'Tis a pageant
	To keep us in false gaze. When we consider
	Th' importancy of Cyprus to the Turk, 20
	And let ourselves again but understand
	That, as it more concerns the Turk than Rhodes,
	So may he with more facile question bear it,
	For that it stands not in such warlike brace,
	But altogether lacks th' abilities 25
	That Rhodes is dressed in—if we make thought of this,
	We must not think the Turk is so unskillful
	To leave that latest which concerns him first,
	Neglecting an attempt of ease and gain
	To wake and wage a danger profitless. 30
DUKE	Nay, in all confidence he's not for Rhodes.
OFFICER	Here is more news.
	[Enter a Messenger]
MESSENGER	The Ottomites, reverend and gracious,
	Steering with due course toward the isle of Rhodes,
	Have there injointed them with an after fleet. 35
SENATOR	Ay, so I thought. How many, as you guess?
MESSENGER	Of thirty sail; and now they do restem
	Their backward course, bearing with frank appearance
	Their purposes toward Cyprus. Signior Montano,
	Your trusty and most valiant servitor, 40
	With his free duty recommends you thus,
	And prays you to believe him.
DUKE	'Tis certain then for Cyprus.
	Marcus Luccicos, is not he in town?
1. SENATOR	He's now in Florence. 45
DUKE	Write from us to him; post, post-haste dispatch.
	[Enter BRABANTIO, OTHELLO, CASSIO, IAGO, RODERIGO, and
	Officers]

ACT I

1. SENATOR	This doesn't make sense. It's a trick to draw our attention from Cyprus. When we realize how crucial the island of Cyprus is to the Turks and compare the value of Cyprus to that of Rhodes, Rhodes is more easily captured because it is less fortified and lacks the military readiness. We must not underestimate the Turks and stop guarding Cyprus, the prime target.
DUKE	I agree, the Turks are not heading for the island of Rhodes.
OFFICER	Here is another report. *[A messenger enters the council chamber.]*
MESSENGER	The Turks, gracious Duke, on the way toward Rhodes joined a second fleet of warships.
1. SENATOR	Just as I guessed. How many warships do you estimate?
MESSENGER	About thirty under sail. They have halted their course toward Rhodes and are heading in battle formation toward Cyprus. Montano, your loyal and bravest warrior, reports this out of duty and asks that you take his word for it.
DUKE	The battle will be for possession of Cyprus. Is Marcus Luccicos available?
1. SENATOR	He has gone to Florence in western Italy.
DUKE	Send a letter to him from me as quickly as possible. *[BRA-BANTIO, OTHELLO, CASSIO, IAGO, RODERIGO, and some officers enter.]*

TRANSLATION

1. SENATOR	Here comes Brabantio and the valiant Moor.
DUKE	Valiant Othello, we must straight employ you Against the general enemy Ottoman. *[To BRABANTIO]* I did not see you. Welcome, gentle signior. 50 We lacked your counsel and your help to-night.
BRABANTIO	So did I yours. Good your grace, pardon me. Neither my place, nor aught I heard of business, Hath raised me from my bed; nor doth the general care Take hold on me; for my particular grief 55 Is of so floodgate and o'erbearing nature That it engluts and swallows other sorrows, And it is still itself.
DUKE	Why, what's the matter?
BRABANTIO	My daughter! O, my daughter!
ALL	Dead?
BRABANTIO	Ay, to me. She is abused, stol'n from me, and corrupted 60 By spells and medicines bought of mountebanks; For nature so prepost'rously to err, Being not deficient, blind, or lame of sense, Sans witchcraft could not.
DUKE	Whoe'er he be that in this foul proceeding 65 Hath thus beguiled your daughter of herself, And you of her, the bloody book of law You shall yourself read in the bitter letter After your own sense; yea, though our proper son Stood in your action. 70
BRABANTIO	Humbly I thank your grace. Here is the man—this Moor, whom now, it seems, Your special mandate for the state affairs Hath hither brought.

1. SENATOR	Here come Brabantio and the brave Othello.
DUKE	Gallant Othello, we need you immediately to fight off the warlike Turks. *[To BRABANTIO]* I didn't notice you. Welcome, kind sir. We needed your advice and assistance at our meeting tonight.
BRABANTIO	And I needed your advice and assistance. Good sir, excuse me. It wasn't my civic post nor news of danger that dragged me out of bed, nor was it concern for public safety. My personal sorrow is so overflowing and heavy that it easily overwhelms other griefs.
DUKE	What is the problem?
BRABANTIO	My daughter! Oh, my daughter!
ALL	Is she dead?
BRABANTIO	Yes, to me she seems dead. She was tricked, whisked away from home, and deceived by magic spells and potions bought from drug dealers. Nature, which is not lacking in reason, could not make so great an error unless some evil spell were involved.
DUKE	Whoever did this cruel deed has deceived your daughter of her sense and robbed you of her. You shall interpret the law yourself, even if my own son were the guilty man.
BRABANTIO	I humbly thank you. Here is the villain, this black man, whom you have summoned on military matters.

ACT I

TRANSLATION

ALL	We are very sorry for't.
DUKE	*[To OTHELLO]* What, in your own part, can you say to this?
BRABANTIO	Nothing, but this is so. 75
OTHELLO	Most potent, grave, and reverend signiors,

OTHELLO

Most potent, grave, and reverend signiors,
My very noble, and approved good masters,
That I have ta'en away this old man's daughter,
It is most true; true I have married her.
The very head and front of my offending   80
Hath this extent, no more. Rude am I in my speech,
And little blessed with the soft phrase of peace;
For since these arms of mine had seven years' pith
Till now some nine moons wasted, they have used
Their dearest action in the tented field;   85
And little of this great world can I speak
More than pertains to feats of broil and battle;
And therefore little shall I grace my cause
In speaking for myself. Yet, by your gracious patience,
I will a round unvarnished tale deliver   90
Of my whole course of love—what drugs, what charms,
What conjuration, and what mighty magic
(For such proceeding am I charged withal)
I won his daughter.

BRABANTIO

                    A maiden never bold;
Of spirit so still and quiet that her motion   95
Blushed at herself; and she—in spite of nature,
Of years, of country, credit, everything—
To fall in love with what she feared to look on!
It is a judgment maimed and most imperfect
That will confess perfection so could err.   100
Against all rules of nature, and must be driven
To find out practices of cunning hell
Why this should be. I therefore vouch again
That with some mixtures pow'rful o'er the blood,
Or with some dram, conjured to this effect,   105
He wrought upon her.

ALL	We are sorry for your suffering.
DUKE	*[To OTHELLO]* What do you have to say in your own defense?
BRABANTIO	He can say nothing, because the charge is true.
OTHELLO	Most powerful, serious, and respected gentlemen, all noble and honored wisemen, it is true that I have taken this old man's daughter. It is true that I married her. The extent of my fault is only marrying her, nothing else. I am not an educated speaker or gifted with pretty words; until nine months ago, I had been a soldier in the field for a span of seven years. I don't know much about the world beyond battlefield courage. I have little to say to build a case for myself. If you will be patient, I will tell you straight what drugs, what magic spells, what sorcery and magic (for which Brabantio charges me) I employed to court his daughter.
BRABANTIO	She is a shy maiden so subdued and silent that she blushes at her own actions. In spite of her shyness, age, patriotism, good name, and everything else, she fell in love with the kind of person who would terrify her! Only faulty logic could justify so unwise, so abnormal a decision. We must investigate the hellish plot that won her love. I declare once more that some potion or drug overpowered her and caused this love match that he used to win her.

TRANSLATION

DUKE   To vouch this is no proof,
Without more certain and more overt test
Than these thin habits and poor likelihoods
Of modern seeming do prefer against him.

1. SENATOR   But, Othello, speak.   110
Did you by indirect and forced courses
Subdue and poison this young maid's affections?
Or came it by request, and such fair question
As soul to soul affordeth?

OTHELLO   I do beseech you,
Send for the lady to the Sagittary   115
And let her speak of me before her father.
If you do find me foul in her report,
The trust, the office, I do hold of you
Not only take away, but let your sentence
Even fall upon my life.   120

DUKE   Fetch Desdemona hither.

OTHELLO   Ancient, conduct them; you best know the place.
[Exit IAGO, with two or three Attendants]
And till she come, as truly as to heaven
I do confess the vices of my blood,
So justly to your grave ears I'll present
How I did thrive in this fair lady's love,   125
And she in mine.

DUKE   Say it, Othello.

DUKE   Saying is not proving. I need a test of these flimsy accusations and poor conclusions that Othello is guilty.

1. SENATOR   Tell us, Othello. Did you by devious means or force seize and twist this young girl's emotions? Or did you win her by a normal question, the kind that one person might ask another?

OTHELLO   Please send for her at the Archer Inn and let her testify in front of her father of her feelings for me. If she says I am guilty, then take away my reputation and my military post and sentence me to death.

DUKE   Bring Desdemona to the Duke's chambers.

OTHELLO   Flag bearer, lead the way; you know where she is. *[IAGO departs with two or three men.]* Until she arrives, I will confess my faults before God. To this council I will explain how I basked in her love and Desdemona in mine.

DUKE   Tell us, Othello.

TRANSLATION

OTHELLO	Her father loved me, oft invited me;	
	Still questioned me the story of my life	
	From year to year—the battles, sieges, fortunes	130
	That I have passed.	
	I ran it through, even from my boyish days	
	To th' very moment that he bade me tell it.	
	Wherein I spake of most disastrous chances,	
	Of moving accidents by flood and field;	135
	Of hairbreadth scapes i' th' imminent deadly breach;	
	Of being taken by the insolent foe	
	And sold to slavery; of my redemption thence	
	And portance in my travel's history;	
	Wherein of anters vast and deserts idle,	140
	Rough quarries, rocks, and hills whose heads touch heaven	
	It was my hint to speak—such was the process;	
	And of the Cannibals that each other eat,	
	The Anthropophagi, and men whose heads	
	Do grow beneath their shoulders. This to hear	145
	Would Desdemona seriously incline;	
	But still the house affairs would draw her thence;	
	Which ever as she could with haste dispatch,	
	She'ld come again, and with a greedy ear	
	Devour up my discourse. Which I observing,	150
	Took once a pliant hour, and found good means	
	To draw from her a prayer of earnest heart	
	That I would all my pilgrimage dilate,	
	Whereof by parcels she had something heard,	
	But not intentively. I did consent	155
	And often did beguile her of her tears	
	When I did speak of some distressful stroke	
	That my youth suffered. My story being done,	
	She gave me for my pains a world of sighs.	
	She swore, i' faith, 'twas strange, 'twas passing strange;	160
	'Twas pitiful, 'twas wondrous pitiful.	
	She wished she had not heard it; yet she wished	
	That heaven had made her such a man. She thanked me;	
	And bade me, if I had a friend that loved her,	
	I should but teach him how to tell my story,	165
	And that would woo her. Upon this hint I spake.	
	She loved me for the dangers I had passed,	
	And I loved her that she did pity them.	
	This only is the witchcraft I have used.	
	Here comes the lady. Let her witness it.	170
	[Enter DESDEMONA, IAGO, Attendants]	

OTHELLO   Brabantio approved of me and often made me his guest. He liked to hear about my past and the time line of my battles and attacks and of the good luck that has come my way. I recited everything, from my childhood to the moment of my arrival at his house. I revealed my most dangerous risks, the events on sea and land, and near-death experiences. I told of my capture and sale as a slave, of my rescue and my conduct during long travels. I described my wanderings in deep caves and empty deserts, over crags, rocks, and hills as tall as the sky. I told about cannibals and man-eaters and of men whose heads are in their chests. Desdemona leaned attentively toward me while I recited my stories. When she had household duties, she completed her chores and hurried back to listen again to my adventures. I noticed her interest. I spoke in private with her and learned that she wanted to hear more of my journeys that I had already described in parts. I agreed to tell her more and moved her to tears when I recounted some hardship from my youth. When I finished talking, she rewarded me with sighs. She declared my adventures strange and pitiable. She wished that she had not heard so sad a tale. She wished that God would send her a man like me. She thanked me and requested that, if I had a friend who admired her, I should instruct him in the art of storytelling as a form of courtship. I took this as an opportunity to speak for myself. She loved me for the troubles of my past and I loved her for her sympathy. These stories are the only sorcery I have used to win her. Here she comes. Let her attest to what I said. *[DESDEMONA, IAGO, and servants enter the Duke's chambers.]*

ACT I

DUKE	I think this tale would win my daughter too.
	Good Brabantio,
	Take up this mangled matter at the best.
	Men do their broken weapons rather use
	Than their bare hands. 175
BRABANTIO	I pray you hear her speak.
	If she confess that she was half the wooer,
	Destruction on my head if my bad blame
	Light on the man! Come thither, gentle mistress.
	Do you perceive in all this noble company
	Where most you owe obedience? 180
DESDEMONA	My noble father,
	I do perceive here a divided duty.
	To you I am bound for life and education;
	My life and education both do learn me
	How to respect you: you are the lord of duty;
	I am hitherto your daughter. But here's my husband; 185
	And so much duty as my mother showed
	To you, preferring you before her father,
	So much I challenge that I may profess
	Due to the Moor my lord.
BRABANTIO	God b' wi' ye! I have done.
	Please it your grace, on to the state affairs. 190
	I had rather to adopt a child than get it.
	Come hither, Moor.
	I here do give thee that with all my heart
	Which, but thou hast already, with all my heart
	I would keep from thee. For your sake, jewel, 195
	I am glad at soul I have no other child;
	For thy escape would teach me tyranny,
	To hang clogs on them. I have done, my lord.
DUKE	Let me speak like yourself and lay a sentence
	Which, as a grise or step, may help these lovers 200
	(Into your favor.)
	When remedies are past, the griefs are ended
	By seeing the worst, which late on hopes depended.
	To mourn a mischief that is past and gone
	Is the next way to draw new mischief on. 205
	What cannot be preserved when fortune takes,
	Patience her injury a mock'ry makes.
	The robbed that smiles steals something from the thief;
	He robs himself that spends a bootless grief.

ORIGINAL

DUKE	I think my daughter would also choose this storyteller for a husband. Brabantio, try to mend this rift between your daughter and her new husband. People prefer imperfect means to an end rather than violence.
BRABANTIO	I beg you to hear Desdemona's side of the story. If she claims to have encouraged Othello's courtship, sentence me for the charges I have raised against Othello. Come here, sweet lady. To whom in this worthy group do you owe the most loyalty?
DESDEMONA	Good father, I must make a choice. I am grateful to you for giving me life and training. From experience and education I have learned about respecting my parent. You control my obligations. I obey you as a daughter should. But Othello is my husband. Just as my mother obeyed you rather than remain in her father's household, so I declare my allegiance to Othello, my master.
BRABANTIO	Off with you! I give up. If the Duke wishes, let's return to state business. I would rather adopt a stranger than sire a child. Come here, black man. I sincerely offer you my daughter, whom you've already married, the one thing I would rather deny you. Because of this elopement, my precious gem, I am glad I have no other child to lose. This hasty marriage would make me cruel enough to tie weights to my other children. I am finished, my lord.
DUKE	I wish to speak to this couple like a father and to offer a challenge to help them gain your approval. When it is too late to prevent an elopement, worries of the worst that could happen are useless. To continue grieving over a misadventure will only cause more family trouble. When luck destroys hope, tolerance overcomes the hurt. The outraged father's acceptance of Othello ends charges of crime. Anyone who continues complaining about the past robs himself of contentment.

BRABANTIO	So let the Turk of Cyprus us beguile:	210
	We lose it not so long as we can smile.	
	He bears the sentence well that nothing bears	
	But the free comfort which from thence he hears;	
	But he bears both the sentence and the sorrow	
	That to pay grief must of poor patience borrow.	215
	These sentences, to sugar, or to gall,	
	Being strong on both sides, are equivocal.	
	But words are words. I never yet did hear	
	That the bruised heart was pierced through the ear.	
	Beseech you, now to the affairs of state.	220
DUKE	The Turk with a most mighty preparation	
	makes for Cyprus. Othello, the fortitude of the	
	place is best known to you; and though we have	
	there a substitute of most allowed sufficiency, yet	
	opinion, a sovereign mistress of effects, throws a	225
	more safer voice on you. You must therefore be	
	content to slubber the gloss of your new fortunes	
	with this more stubborn and boisterous expedition.	
OTHELLO	The tyrant custom, most grave senators,	
	Hath made the flinty and steel couch of war	230
	My thrice-driven bed of down. I do agnise	
	A natural and prompt alacrity	
	I find in hardness; and do undertake	
	These present wars against the Ottomites.	
	Most humbly, therefore, bending to your state,	235
	I crave fit disposition for my wife,	
	Due reference of place, and exhibition,	
	With such accommodation and besort	
	As levels with her breeding.	
DUKE	If you please,	
	Be't at her father's.	240
BRABANTIO	I'll not have it so.	
OTHELLO	Nor I.	

BRABANTIO	Then let the Turks cheat us out of the island of Cyprus. It won't hurt us if we can be happy about it. The best way to endure a hardship is to accept friendly advice in place of revenge. Anyone who endures both punishment and hurt must borrow patience to tolerate grief. These judgments—whether soothing or harsh—have the same value. Words are only words. I have never heard it said that a surgeon can treat a broken heart by poking through the ear. Please, let's get back to business.
DUKE	The Turks have amassed a force to move against Cyprus. Othello, you know better than anyone how well the island is fortified. I have sent a dependable military leader, but others think that you are a better choice of adviser. You must agree to withdraw from your honeymoon and take charge of this difficult naval expedition to Cyprus.
OTHELLO	It is the nature of war, gentlemen, to offer me weapons in place of an extra-soft feather bed. Because of my combat experience, I accept the hardship of immediate battle. I agree to fight the war for Venice against the Turks. Humbly before the Duke, I ask for housing for my wife and appropriate treatment suited to her refined social position.
DUKE	If it suits you, let Desdemona stay at her father's house.
BRABANTIO	I won't have her in the house.
OTHELLO	Nor will I allow it.

DESDEMONA	Nor I. I would not there reside,
	To put my father in impatient thoughts
	By being in his eye. Most gracious Duke,
	To my unfolding lend your prosperous ear,
	And let me find a charter in your voice, 245
	To assist my simpleness.
DUKE	What would you, Desdemona?
DESDEMONA	That I did love the Moor to live with him,
	My downright violence, and storm of fortunes,
	May trumpet to the world. My heart's subdued 250
	Even to the very quality of my lord.
	I saw Othello's visage in his mind,
	And to his honors and his valiant parts
	Did I my soul and fortunes consecrate.
	So that, dear lords, if I be left behind, 255
	A moth of peace, and he go to the war,
	The rites for which I love him are bereft me,
	And I a heavy interim shall support
	By his dear absence. Let me go with him.
OTHELLO	Let her have your voices. 260
	Vouch with me, heaven, I therefore beg it not
	To please the palate of my appetite,
	Nor to comply with heat—the young affects
	In me defunct—and proper satisfaction;
	But to be free and bounteous to her mind; 265
	And heaven defend your good souls that you think
	I will your serious and great business scant
	For she is with me. No, when light-winged toys
	Of feathered Cupid seel with wanton dullness
	My speculative and officed instruments, 270
	That my disports corrupt and taint my business,
	Let housewives make a skillet of my helm,
	And all indign and base adversities
	Make head against my estimation!

DESDEMONA   I also disagree. I would not annoy my father further by remaining in his presence. Gracious Duke, hear my simple request for your permission.

DUKE   What do you propose, Desdemona?

DESDEMONA   I will shout to the world that I love the black man, that I live with him in spite of causing trouble for my father by eloping. My heart belongs to Othello, even if he is a professional soldier. I fell in love with his character and pledged myself, heart and soul, to a brave and honorable warrior. Dear sirs, if I stay home and he goes to fight, I betray my reason for loving him. Our time apart would weigh heavily on me. Let me accompany him to war.

OTHELLO   Give her your reply. I promise by God that I beg to take her with me not for sexual lust, which I have already satisfied. Speak generously to her proposal. Don't assume that I will shirk my military responsibilities if she accompanies me toward Cyprus. If lovesickness blind me to my sea duties and weapons and lovemaking ruin my soldiery, let housewives turn my helmet into a frying pan; let shame attack my reputation.

DUKE	Be it as you shall privately determine,	275
	Either for her stay or going. Th' affair cries haste,	
	And speed must answer it.	
1. SENATOR	You must away to-night.	
OTHELLO	With all my heart.	

DUKE At nine i' th' morning here we'll meet again.
Othello, leave some officer behind, 280
And he shall our commission bring to you,
With such things else of quality and respect
As doth import you.

OTHELLO   So please your grace, my ancient;
A man he is of honesty and trust.
To his conveyance I assign my wife, . 285
With what else needful your good grace shall think
To be sent after me.

DUKE   Let it be so.
Good night to every one. *[To BRABANTIO]* And, noble signior,
If virtue no delighted beauty lack,
Your son-in-law is far more fair than black. 290

1. SENATOR Adieu, brave Moor. Use Desdemona well.

BRABANTIO Look to her, Moor, if thou hast eyes to see:
She has deceived her father, and may thee.
[Exeunt DUKE, Senators, Officers, etc.]

OTHELLO My life upon her faith!—Honest Iago,
My Desdemona must I leave to thee. 295
I prithee let thy wife attend on her,
And bring them after in the best advantage.
Come, Desdemona. I have but an hour
Of love, of worldly matters and direction,
To spend with thee. We must obey the time. 300
[Exeunt MOOR and DESDEMONA]

DUKE	Choose for yourself whether she stays or goes with you. The situation demands speed. You must hurry on your away.
1. SENATOR	You must sail tonight.
OTHELLO	I'll do my best.
DUKE	We will convene this council again at 9:00 in the morning. Othello, post an officer here. He will convey our instructions to you as well as anything else you need for war.
OTHELLO	If you agree, I will leave my flag bearer Iago, an honest, trustworthy man. I leave Desdemona in his care with whatever else you intend to send me.
DUKE	So be it. Good night, everyone. *[To BRABANTIO]* Noble sir, if virtue can be beautiful, your son-in-law is more handsome than black.
1. SENATOR	God go with you, brave Othello. Take good care of Desdemona.
BRABANTIO	Be careful, black man, and keep your eye on her. She tricked her father; she may trick you. *[The DUKE, senators, officers, and the rest go out.]*
OTHELLO	I pledge my life for her trust in me! Trusty Iago, I must leave Desdemona in your care. Please have your wife watch over her and bring the two women along when you have the opportunity. Come with me, Desdemona. I have one hour for love and for personal pleasures. We must use what time we have. *[The black man and DESDEMONA go out.]*

RODERIGO	Iago,—
IAGO	What say'st thou, noble heart?
RODERIGO	What will I do, think'st thou?
IAGO	Why, go to bed and sleep.
RODERIGO	I will incontinently drown myself. 305

IAGO   If thou dost, I shall never love thee after.
Why, thou silly gentleman!

RODERIGO   It is silliness to live when to live is torment;
and then have we a prescription to die when
death is our physician. 310

IAGO   O villainous! I have looked upon the world
for four times seven years; and since I could
distinguish betwixt a benefit and an injury, I never
found man that knew how to love himself. Ere I would
say I would drown myself for the love of a guinea 315
hen, I would change my humanity with a baboon.

RODERIGO   What should I do? I confess it is my
shame to be so fond, but it is not in my virtue to
amend it.

IAGO   Virtue? a fig! 'Tis in ourselves that we are 320
thus or thus. Our bodies are our gardens, to the
which our wills are gardeners; so that if we will
plant nettles or sow lettuce, set hyssop and weed up
thyme, supply it with one gender of herbs or distract
it with many—either to have it sterile with 325
idleness or manured with industry—why, the
power and corrigible authority of this lies in our
wills. If the balance of our lives had not one scale
of reason to poise another of sensuality, the blood
and baseness of our natures would conduct us to 330
most preposterous conclusions. But we have reason
to cool our raging motions, our carnal stings, our
unbitted lusts; whereof I take this that you call love
to be a sect or scion.

RODERIGO   It cannot be. 335

RODERIGO	Iago—
IAGO	What did you say, good sir?
RODERIGO	What should I do? What do you think?
IAGO	You should go to bed and sleep.
RODERIGO	I will drown myself at once.
IAGO	If you do, I will lose all admiration for you. Don't be silly!
RODERIGO	It is more foolish to live in torment when I could be my own healer and kill myself.
IAGO	What an evil thought! I am 28 years old and know the difference between help and harm. I have never met a person who knew how to treat himself well. Before I would drown myself over love of a peahen, I would rather be a monkey.
RODERIGO	What should I do? I admit it is shameful to be so lovesick, but it is not in my character to give up on her.
IAGO	Character is not worth a fig. We will ourselves to be what we are. Our bodies are like gardens that we actively cultivate. If we choose to plant stickers rather than lettuce seeds, to set sweet-smelling herbs and pull up thyme, stock up on one type of herb or plant a variety, to leave the ground unplanted or to work busily at fertilizing, why, it is our own choice. If we don't balance our behavior with logic on one side and romance on the other, our lustful nature would direct us to absurd misadventures. Instead, we use sanity to control raging emotions, our bodily urges, our unrestrained desires. I think what you call "love" is only a twig of the whole tree.
RODERIGO	You can't be right.

IAGO	It is merely a lust of the blood and a permission
	of the will. Come, be a man! Drown thyself?
	Drown cats and blind puppies! I have professed
	me thy friend, and I confess me knit to thy deserving
	with cables of perdurable toughness. I could	340
	never better stead thee than now. Put money in thy
	purse. Follow these wars; defeat thy favor with an
	usurped beard. I say, put money in thy purse. It
	cannot be that Desdemona should long continue her
	love for the Moor—put money in thy purse—nor	345
	he his to her. It was a violent commencement, and
	thou shalt see an answerable sequestration—put
	but money in thy purse. These Moors are changeable
	in their wills—fill thy purse with money. The
	food that to him now is as luscious as locusts shall	350
	be to him shortly as bitter as coloquintida. She
	must change for youth: when she is sated with his
	body, she will find the error of her choice. (She must
	have change, she must.) Therefore put money in thy
	purse. If thou wilt needs damn thyself, do it a more	355
	delicate way than drowning. Make all the money
	thou canst. If sanctimony and a frail vow betwixt
	an erring barbarian and a supersubtle Venetian
	be not too hard for my wits and all the tribe
	of hell, thou shalt enjoy her. Therefore make	360
	money. A pox of drowning! 'Tis clean out of the
	way. Seek thou rather to be hanged in compassing
	thy joy than to be drowned and go without her.

| RODERIGO | Wilt thou be fast to my hopes, if I depend |
| | on the issue? | 365 |

IAGO	Thou art sure of me. Go, make money. I
	have told thee often, and I retell thee again and
	again, I hate the Moor. My cause is hearted; thine
	hath no less reason. Let us be conjunctive in our
	revenge against him. If thou canst cuckold him,	370
	thou dost thyself a pleasure, me a sport. There
	are many events in the womb of time, which will
	be delivered. Traverse, go, provide thy money!
	We will have more of this to-morrow. Adieu.

| IAGO | You are a victim of sexual desire that you willfully pursue. Act like a man! Why would you drown yourself? People drown only cats and blind puppies. I claim you as my friend and I attach myself to your friendship with durable ties. I could never be a better friend to you than I am now. You can bank on it. Join the fighting force. Grow a beard to cover up your moony looks. You can depend on my advice. I predict that Desdemona will fall out of love with Othello and he will tire of her. Their elopement was hasty. I would bet that a long confinement together will end their love match. Black men are undependable, you can bet on it. The pleasure he now compares to the juicy locust fruit will soon seem as unpalatable as the bitter apple. She will change as she matures. When she grows weary of his body, she will realize her mistake in marrying him. (She will demand variety, she must.) You can bet on my prediction. If you have to doom yourself, choose an easier way than drowning. Live as fully as you can. If holiness and a marriage vow between a wandering alien and a refined Venetian girl don't repulse you and everyone in hell, you will some day have her for your own. Make the most of opportunity. Drowning yourself is nonsense! It's completely wrong-headed thinking. Choose to risk execution for satisfying your desire than to kill yourself and lose all hope of her. |

| RODERIGO | Will you remain loyal to my desires, if I rely on the outcome of your advice? |

| IAGO | You can rely on me. You can bank on it. I have told you frequently and I tell you again, I hate the black man. My anger is heartfelt; you have no less reason to hate Othello. Let us unite and seek vengeance on him. If you can seduce Desdemona, you will enjoy the act and I will enjoy the challenge. There are opportunities waiting for their time to happen. Go on, take a chance! We will talk more tomorrow. God go with you. |

RODERIGO	Where shall we meet i' th' morning?	375
IAGO	At my lodging.	
RODERIGO	I'll be with thee betimes.	
IAGO	Go to, farewell.—Do you hear, Roderigo?	
RODERIGO	What say you?	
IAGO	No more of drowning, do you hear?	380
RODERIGO	I am changed.	
IAGO	Go to, farewell. Put money enough in your purse.	
RODERIGO	I'll sell all my land. *[Exit]*	

IAGO Thus do I ever make my fool my purse;　375 385
For I mine own gained knowledge should profane
If I would time expend with such a snipe
But for my sport and profit. I hate the Moor;
And it is thought abroad that 'twixt my sheets
Was done my office. I know not if't be true;　390
Yet I, for mere suspicion in that kind,
Will do as if for surety. He holds me well;
The better shall my purpose work on him.
Cassio's a proper man. Let me see now;
To get his place, and to plume up my will　395
In double knavery—How, how?—Let's see:—
After some time, to abuse Othello's ear
That he is too familiar with his wife.
He hath a person and a smooth dispose
To be suspected—framed to make women false.　400
The Moor is of a free and open nature
That thinks men honest that but seem to be so;
And will as tenderly be led by th' nose
As asses are.
I have't! It is engendered! Hell and night　405
Must bring this monstrous birth to the world's light. *[Exit]*

RODERIGO	Where shall we meet tomorrow morning?
IAGO	At my room.
RODERIGO	I'll see you then.
IAGO	Okay, goodbye. By the way, Roderigo?
RODERIGO	What's that?
IAGO	I warn you, don't think any more about suicide.
RODERIGO	I've given up the thought.
IAGO	Okay, goodbye. Be ready to win this bet.

RODERIGO   I will sell my property. *[He goes out.]*

IAGO   I often profit from tricking fools. I would waste my time by loitering with such a nitwit except for fun and financial gain. I hate the black man; there is a rumor that I achieved my promotion through sexual favors. I don't know if that charge is true. I will accept the suspicion and act as though it is fact. Othello likes me. His favor will help me gain vengeance against him. Cassio's an attractive choice. Let me think about it. How can I help him get what he wants and achieve my dirty work in a double trick. Let's see. After a pause, I will hint to Othello that Cassio flirts with Desdemona. Cassio is handsome and smooth enough for Othello to suspect him of seduction. The black man is so open and naive that he believes that anybody who acts honest is trustworthy. I can lead Othello as gently by the nose as a donkey. I know what I'll do! I have a plan! My evil plot will develop in hellish darkness before it comes to light. *[He goes out.]*

ACT II, SCENE 1

A seaport in Cyprus. An open place near the quay.

[Enter MONTANO and two Gentlemen]

MONTANO	What from the cape can you discern at sea?

1. GENTLEMAN   Nothing at all: it is a high-wrought flood.
I cannot 'twixt the heaven and the main
Descry sail.

MONTANO   Methinks the wind hath spoke aloud at land;   5
A fuller blast ne'er shook our battlements.
If it hath ruffianed so upon the sea,
What ribs of oak, when mountains melt on them,
Can hold the mortise? What shall we hear of this?

2. GENTLEMAN   A segregation of the Turkish fleet.   10
For do but stand upon the foaming shore,
The chidden billow seems to pelt the clouds;
The wind-shaked surge, with high and monstrous mane,
Seems to cast water on the burning Bear
And quench the Guards of th' ever-fixed pole.   15
I never did like molestation view
On the enchafed flood.

MONTANO   If that the Turkish fleet
Be not ensheltered and embayed, they are drowned;
It is impossible they bear it out.
[Enter a third Gentleman]

3. GENTLEMAN   News, lads! Our wars are done.   20
The desperate tempest hath so banged the Turks
That their designment halts. A noble ship of Venice
Has seen a grievous wrack and sufferance
On most part of their fleet.

MONTANO   How? Is this true?   25

3. GENTLEMAN   The ship is here put in,
A Veronesa; Michael Cassio,
Lieutenant to the warlike Moor Othello,
Is come on shore; the Moor himself at sea,
And is in full commission here for Cyprus.

ACT II, SCENE 1

A seaport on the island of Cyprus.

[MONTANO and two gentlemen enter.]

MONTANO   Can you spot anything at sea by looking out from this point?

1. GENTLEMAN   I can't see a thing. The sea is too rough. I can't make out a sail between the sky and the water.

MONTANO   I think the wind had its say on land. Our fort has never been so shaken before. If the wind was as rough at sea, how could oak beams hold fast when mountains of water fall on them? What will we learn about this battle?

2. GENTLEMAN   The disbanding of the Turkish navy. We are standing on firm beach and witnessing the waves hitting the sky. The gale-blown tide, high and fearful, seems to hurl water on the Big Dipper and to blow out two stars from the constellation. I've never seen the ocean so violent.

MONTANO   If the Turkish navy didn't anchor in a port, the men have drowned. They could not have ridden out this storm at sea. *[A third gentleman enters.]*

3. GENTLEMAN   I bring news, boys! The war is over. The rough seas have so battered the Turkish navy that they have given up. A valiant Venetian ship has survived terrible buffeting and avoided the damage that hit most of the fleet.

MONTANO   Really! Is this true?

3. GENTLEMAN   The lead ship, a vessel made in Verona, has arrived in port. Michael Cassio, Othello's lieutenant, has gone ashore. Othello himself, admiral of the fleet, is on the way to Cyprus.

MONTANO	I am glad on't. 'Tis a worthy governor.	30

3. GENTLEMAN   But this same Cassio, though he speak of comfort
Touching the Turkish loss, yet he looks sadly
And prays the Moor be safe, for they were parted
With foul and violent tempest.

MONTANO   Pray heaven he be;
For I have served him, and the man commands   35
Like a full soldier. Let's to the seaside, ho!
As well to see the vessel that's come in
As to throw out our eyes for brave Othello,
Even till we make the main and th' aerial blue
An indistinct regard.   40

3. GENTLEMAN   Come, let's do so;
For every minute is expectancy
Of more arrivance.
[Enter CASSIO]

CASSIO   Thanks, you the valiant of this warlike isle,
That so approve the Moor! O, let the heavens
Give him defense against the elements,   45
For I have lost him on a dangerous sea!

MONTANO   Is he well shipped?

CASSIO   His bark is stoutly timbered, and his pilot
Of very expert and approved allowance;
Therefore my hopes, not surfeited to death,   50
Stand in bold cure. *[Within]* A sail, a sail, a sail!
[Enter a Messenger]

CASSIO   What noise?

MESSENGER   The town is empty; on the brow o' th' sea
Stand ranks of people, and they cry 'A sail!'

CASSIO   My hopes do shape him for the governor.   55
[A shot]

2. GENTLEMAN   They do discharge their shot of courtesy:
Our friends at least.

CASSIO   I pray you, sir, go forth
And give us truth who 'tis that is arrived.

2. GENTLEMAN   I shall. *[Exit]*

MONTANO	I am glad to hear it. Othello is a worthy governor.
3. GENTLEMAN	Cassio is glad that the Turks have withdrawn, but he worries about Othello's safety. The two soldiers were separated by turbulent seas.
MONTANO	Heaven keep Othello safe. I have served under him. He commands like a true soldier. Let's hurry to the beach! We can see what vessel has docked and look for brave Othello, even if we can't detect a break between water and sky.
3. GENTLEMAN	Let's go. Every minute, more ships may arrive. *[CASSIO enters.]*
CASSIO	Thanks to the daring people of Cyprus for supporting Othello! Oh, let God defend him from the storm, for I lost sight of him in the roaring sea!
MONTANO	Is his ship stout?
CASSIO	His vessel is securely built and his navigator is an expert at sea combat. I trust that my hopes overcome my fears of Othello's death. *[Offstage]* We spot a sail! *[A messenger enters.]*
CASSIO	What was the commotion?
MESSENGER	Everyone in town ran to the beach and announced sight of a sail.
CASSIO	I hope the people make Othello their governor. *[A shot sounds.]*
2. GENTLEMAN	They fire a welcome salute in friendship.
CASSIO	Please, sir, go ahead and return with a report on who has arrived.
2. GENTLEMAN	I shall. *[The gentleman goes out.]*

ACT II

MONTANO	But, good lieutenant, is your general wived? 60
CASSIO	Most fortunately. He hath achieved a maid That paragons description and wild fame; One that excels the quirks of blazoning pens, And in th' essential vesture of creation Does tire the ingener. 65 *[Enter Second Gentleman]* How now? Who has put in?
2. GENTLEMAN	'Tis one Iago, ancient to the general.
CASSIO	H'as had most favorable and happy speed: Tempests themselves, high seas, and howling winds, The guttered rocks and congregated sands, Traitors ensteeped to clog the guiltless keel 70 As having sense of beauty, do omit Their mortal natures, letting go safely by The divine Desdemona.
MONTANO	What is she?
CASSIO	She that I spake of, our great captain's captain, Left in the conduct of the bold Iago, 75 Whose footing here anticipates our thoughts A se'nnight's speed. Great Jove, Othello guard, And swell his sail with thine own pow'rful breath, That he may bless this bay with his tall ship, Make love's quick pants in Desdemona's arms, 80 Give renewed fire to our extinct spirits, (And bring all Cyprus comfort!). *[Enter DESDEMONA, IAGO, RODERIGO, and EMILIA with Attendants]* O, behold! The riches of the ship is come on shore! Ye men of Cyprus, let her have your knees. Hail to thee, lady! and the grace of heaven, 85 Before, behind thee, and on every hand, Enwheel thee round!
DESDEMONA	I thank you, valiant Cassio. What tidings can you tell me of my lord?
CASSIO	He is not yet arrived; nor know I aught But that he's well and will be shortly here. 90

MONTANO	Lieutenant Cassio, is General Othello married?
CASSIO	He is well matched. He has married a young woman who is even more perfect than her description or rumors. She outranks written summaries. Her qualities weary the person who tries to flatter her. [*The second gentleman enters.*] What has happened? Who has docked?
2. GENTLEMAN	It is Iago, General Othello's flag bearer.
CASSIO	He has had luck in arriving so fast. Storms, breakers, and gales, jagged rocks and sand dunes that entrap the ship's bottom are so aware of Desdemona's beauty that they let her go by unharmed.
MONTANO	Who is Desdemona?
CASSIO	The woman I spoke of, General Othello's bride, left in the care of Iago who anchors after a speedy week at sea. Jupiter, protect Othello. Blow your breath into his sails that he may steer his great ship to this harbor. Let Othello love Desdemona once more and renew our flagging spirits. (And comfort the people of Cyprus!) [*DESDEMONA, IAGO, RODERIGO, and EMILIA enter with servants.*] Oh, look! The ship's rich company disembarks! Men of Cyprus, kneel to Desdemona. Welcome, lady! God's grace encircle you in front, behind, and all around.
DESDEMONA	Thank you, brave Cassio. What news do you have of Othello?
CASSIO	He has not arrived. I know nothing more than that he survived and will soon reach Cyprus.

ACT II

TRANSLATION

DESDEMONA	O but I fear! How lost you company?
CASSIO	The great contention of the sea and skies Parted our fellowship. <div align="right">*[Within]* A sail, a sail! *[A shot]*</div><div align="right">But hark. A sail!</div>
2. GENTLEMAN	They give their greeting to the citadel; This likewise is a friend. 95
CASSIO	<div align="right">See for the news.</div>*[Exit Gentlemen]* Good ancient, you are welcome. *[To EMILIA]* Welcome, mistress.— Let it not gall your patience, good Iago, That I extend my manners. 'Tis my breeding That gives me this bold show of courtesy. *[Kisses EMILIA]*
IAGO	Sir, would she give you so much of her lips 100 As of her tongue she oft bestows on me, You would have enough.
DESDEMONA	<div align="right">Alas, she has no speech!</div>
IAGO	In faith, too much. I find it still when I have list to sleep. Marry, before your ladyship, I grant, 105 She puts her tongue a little in her heart And chides with thinking.
EMILIA	You have little cause to say so.
IAGO	Come on, come on! You are pictures out of doors. Bells in your parlors, wildcats in your kitchen, 110 Saints in your injuries, devils being offended, Players in your housewifery, and housewives in your beds.
DESDEMONA	O, fie upon thee, slanderer!
IAGO	Nay, it is true, or else I am a Turk: You rise to play, and go to bed to work. 115
EMILIA	You shall not write my praise.
IAGO	<div align="right">No, let me not.</div>
DESDEMONA	What wouldst thou write of me, if thou shouldest praise me?
IAGO	O gentle lady, do not put me to't, For I am nothing if not critical.

ORIGINAL

DESDEMONA	I am afraid to hear it. How were you parted?
CASSIO	The raging ocean and the gale parted our ships. *[Offstage]* A sail! *[A shot is fired.]* Look. A sail!

2. GENTLEMAN	They fire a salute from the fort. This is also a welcome vessel.
CASSIO	Bring us news. *[The gentlemen go out.]* Good flag bearer, we welcome you. *[To EMILIA, IAGO's wife]* Welcome, ma'am. Don't be annoyed, Iago, that I am courteous to Emilia. I was brought up to be openly polite to women. *[CASSIO kisses EMILIA.]*

ACT II

IAGO	Cassio, if she gave you as much of her lips as she gives me harsh words, you would not want any more.
DESDEMONA	But she says nothing!
IAGO	Indeed, she says too much. I can still hear her talking when I want to sleep. Truly, I tell you, Desdemona, Emilia speaks from her heart with thoughts rather than words.
EMILIA	You have no reason to complain.
IAGO	Trust me! Women are beautiful visions on the beach. Clangers in your living rooms, wildcats in the kitchen; you are saints defending your innocence, devils when insulted, triflers at housework, and temptresses in your beds.
DESDEMONA	Oh, hush, liar!
IAGO	But it's true, or else I'm a Turk. You get up to play and go to bed to work.
EMILIA	You won't write my epitaph.
IAGO	No, I don't want to.
DESDEMONA	What would you write about me, if you wanted to praise me?
IAGO	Oh, sweet lady, don't assign me that task, for I am always critical.

TRANSLATION

DESDEMONA	Come on, assay.—There's one gone to the harbor? 120
IAGO	Ay, madam.
DESDEMONA	I am not merry; but I do beguile The thing I am by seeming otherwise.— Come, how wouldst thou praise me?
IAGO	I am about it; but indeed my invention 125 Comes from my pate as birdlime does from frieze— It plucks out brains and all. But my Muse labors, And thus she is delivered: If she be fair and wise, fairness and wit— The one's for use, the other useth it. 130
DESDEMONA	Well praised! How if she be black and witty?
IAGO	If she be black, and thereto have a wit, She'll find a white that shall her blackness fit.
DESDEMONA	Worse and worse!
EMILIA	How if fair and foolish? 135
IAGO	She never yet was foolish that was fair, For even her folly helped her to an heir.
DESDEMONA	These are old fond paradoxes to make fools laugh i' th' alehouse. What miserable praise hast thou for her that's foul and foolish? 140
IAGO	There's none so foul, and foolish thereunto, But does foul pranks which fair and wise ones do.
DESDEMONA	O heavy ignorance! Thou praisest the worst best. But what praise couldst thou bestow on a deserving woman indeed—one that in the 145 authority of her merit did justly put on the vouch of very malice itself?
IAGO	She that was ever fair, and never proud; Had tongue at will, and yet was never loud; Never lacked gold, and yet went never gay; 150 Fled from her wish, and yet said 'Now I may'; She that, being angered, her revenge being nigh, Bade her wrong stay, and her displeasure fly; She that in wisdom never was so frail To change the cod's head for the salmon's tail; 155 She that could think, and ne'er disclose her mind; See suitors following, and not look behind: She was a wight (if ever such wight were)—

DESDEMONA	Go ahead, try it.—Has a ship arrived at the bay?
IAGO	Yes, madam.
DESDEMONA	I am anxious, but I pretend not to worry.—Please, how would you praise me?
IAGO	I'm working on it, but my words stick to my head like adhesive to cloth. The reply yanks out brains and all. My creativity keeps on working and has produced a description: If she is beautiful and smart, beauty and brains—the first is useful, the second uses the first.
DESDEMONA	Well done! What if the woman is ugly and funny?
IAGO	If the woman is ugly and also funny, she will find an opposite to balance her traits.
DESDEMONA	This praise is worse than the first!
EMILIA	Suppose the woman is beautiful and foolish?
IAGO	Women can't be stupid and beautiful at the same time, for even stupidity helps her produce a child.
DESDEMONA	These are the weary sayings that make tipplers laugh at the bar. What wretched praise do you give a woman who is evil-tempered and stupid?
IAGO	No woman is so grumpy and also stupid that she doesn't use the same female trickery that pretty and smart ones use.
DESDEMONA	Oh, ponderous nonsense! You do a better job of praising the worst woman. How would you praise a woman who really deserves admiration—A woman who is so deserving that she could claim good from evil itself?
IAGO	The woman who is always pretty and never conceited; who speaks well but is never loud; who never lacks jewelry, but always dresses tastefully; who never gives in to desires, even when she may indulge them; one who can satisfy her outrage, but who chooses not to seek vengeance. She who is so wise that she would never exchange a valuable fish for a worthless fish tail; she who can reason without revealing her thoughts; she who knows that men admire her, but never looks at them: She is a real person, if ever such a person existed.

TRANSLATION

DESDEMONA	To do what?
IAGO	To suckle fools and chronicle small beer. 160
DESDEMONA	O most lame and impotent conclusion! Do not learn of him, Emilia, though he be thy husband. How say you, Cassio? Is he not a most profane and liberal counsellor?
CASSIO	He speaks home, madam. You may relish 165 him more in the soldier than in the scholar.
IAGO	*[Aside]* He takes her by the palm. Ay, well said, whisper! With as little a web as this will I ensnare as great a fly as Cassio. Ay, smile upon her, do! I will gyve thee in thine own courtship.—You 170 say true; 'tis so, indeed! If such tricks as these strip you out of your lieutenantry, it had been better you had not kissed your three fingers so oft—which now again you are most apt to play the sir in. Very good! well kissed! an excellent curtsy! 'Tis so, 175 indeed. Yet again your fingers to your lips? Would they were clyster pipes for your sake! *[Trumpet within]* The Moor! I know his trumpet.
CASSIO	'Tis truly so.
DESDEMONA	Let's meet him and receive him. 180
CASSIO	Lo, where he comes. *[Enter OTHELLO and Attendants]*
OTHELLO	O my fair warrior!
DESDEMONA	My dear Othello!
OTHELLO	It gives me wonder great as my content To see you here before me. O my soul's joy! If after every tempest come such calms, 185 May the winds blow till they have wakened death! And let the laboring bark climb hills of seas Olympus-high, and duck again so low As hell's from heaven! If it were now to die, 'Twere now to be most happy; for I fear 190 My soul hath her content so absolute That not another comfort like to this Succeeds in unknown fate.

DESDEMONA	To do what?
IAGO	To give birth to stupid babies and total up bar bills.
DESDEMONA	Oh, a pathetic, puny ending! Don't listen to him, Emilia, even if you are married to him. What do you think, Cassio? Isn't Iago the most dishonorable and gushy adviser?
CASSIO	He is blunt, madam. You may find him a better soldier than wise man.
IAGO	*[IAGO to himself]* He holds her hand. Yes, just what I wanted, he whispers to her! With this small fault I will destroy Cassio. Go ahead, smile at Desdemona. I will tie you up in your courtesies. You are right; you tell the truth. If such flirtations as these ruin your career, you would have been wise not to make kissing gestures so often or to play the gallant gentleman. Good! A pretty smooch! An excellent gesture! Very good indeed! You make the same courtly pucker to your fingertips? For your sake, they should be syringe tubes! *[A trumpet sounds offstage.]* Othello! I know his trumpeter.
CASSIO	You're right.
DESDEMONA	Let's meet and welcome him.
CASSIO	Look, here he comes. *[OTHELLO and his company enter.]*
OTHELLO	Hello, beautiful soldier!
DESDEMONA	My dear Othello!
OTHELLO	I am both amazed and pleased to find that you arrived on Cyprus before me. Oh, my soul's joy! If every storm ends so peacefully, I hope the gales blow till that wake up the dead! Let ships climb mountains of water as high as Olympus and drop down as far as hell is from heaven! I could die happy now. I am so satisfied with you that could know no other luxury.

ACT II

TRANSLATION

DESDEMONA   The heavens forbid
But that our loves and comforts should increase
Even as our days grow.   195

OTHELLO   Amen to that, sweet powers!
I cannot speak enough of this content;
It stops me here; it is too much of joy.
And this, and this, the greatest discords be
[They kiss.]
That e'er our hearts shall make!

IAGO   *[Aside]* O, you are well
tuned now!
But I'll set down the pegs that make this music,   200
As honest as I am.

OTHELLO   Come, let us to the castle.
News, friends! Our wars are done; the Turks are drowned.
How does my old acquaintance of this isle?—
Honey, you shall be well desired in Cyprus;
I have found a great love amongst them. O my sweet,   205
I prattle out of fashion, and I dote
In mine own comforts, I prithee, good Iago,
Go to the bay and disembark my coffers.
Bring thou the master to the citadel;
He is a good one, and his worthiness   210
Does challenge much respect.—Come Desdemona,
Once more well met at Cyprus.
[Exeunt OTHELLO all but IAGO and RODERIGO]

IAGO   *[To an Attendant, who goes out]* Do thou
meet me presently at the harbor. *[To RODERIGO]*
Come hither. If thou be'st valiant (as they say base   215
men being in love have then a nobility in their
natures more than is native to them), list me. The
lieutenant to-night watches on the court of guard.
First, I must tell thee this: Desdemona is directly
in love with him.   220

RODERIGO   With him? Why, 'tis not possible.

ORIGINAL

DESDEMONA   God intends for our love and pleasure to increase every day.

OTHELLO   I agree. Heaven's sweet powers bless us! I can't tell you how pleased I am. My words stop from too much happiness. And this kiss and this kiss *[OTHELLO kisses his wife.]* the worst fights we shall ever have.

IAGO   *[IAGO to himself]* Oh, you sing like a well tuned harp! But I will twist the pegs to sound as bluntly as I speak.

OTHELLO   Let's go to the castle. I have good news! The war is over; the Turkish ships sank. How is my old friend on Cyprus? Dear, the people of Cyprus will love you. I have found them very cordial. Sweetheart, I talk too much and I adore my wife. Iago, please go to the harbor and bring my chests. Carry them to the master of the fort. He is worthy and deserving of respect. Come, Desdemona, I am so glad to see you here. *[Everyone leaves with OTHELLO except IAGO and RODERIGO.]*

IAGO   *[To a servant, who departs]* Go to the harbor. I will meet you there shortly. *[To RODERIGO]* Come here. If you be daring (it is said that men in love are more appealing than usual) then listen to me. Lieutenant Cassio has guard duty tonight. I must first inform you that Desdemona loves him.

RODERIGO   She loves Cassio? Impossible!

ACT II

TRANSLATION

IAGO	Lay thy finger thus, and let thy soul be in- structed. Mark me with what violence she first loved the Moor, but for bragging and telling her fantastical lies; and will she love him still for prating? Let not thy discreet heart think it. Her eye must be fed; and what delight shall she have to look on the devil? When the blood is made dull with the act of sport, there should be, again to inflame it and to give satiety a fresh appetite, loveliness in favor, sympathy in years, manners, and beauties; all which the Moor is defective in. Now for want of these required conveniences, her delicate tenderness will find itself abused, begin to heave the gorge, disrelish and abhor the Moor. Very nature will instruct her in it and compel her to some second choice. Now, sir, this granted—as it is a most pregnant and unforced position—who stands so eminent in the degree of this fortune as Cassio does? A knave very voluble; no further conscionable than in putting on the mere form of civil and humane seeming for the better compassing of his salt and most hidden loose affections? Why, none! Why, none! A slipper and subtle knave; a finder-out of occasions; that has an eye can stamp and counterfeit advantages, though true advantage never present itself; a devilish knave! Besides, the knave is handsome, young, and hath all those requisites in him that folly and green minds look after. A pestilent complete knave! and the woman hath found him already.	225 230 235 240 245 250
RODERIGO	I cannot believe that in her; she's full of most blessed condition.	
IAGO	Blessed fig's-end! The wine she drinks is made of grapes. If she had been blessed, she would never have loved the Moor. Blessed pudding! Didst thou not see her paddle with the palm of his hand? Didst not mark that?	255
RODERIGO	Yes, that I did; but that was but courtesy.	

IAGO	Hush and let me explain. Notice how passionately she first loved Othello for bragging and telling lies about his past. Will she keep on loving him for boasting? Don't imagine it. She must see handsome men, but she has only Othello to gaze on. When she is bored with loving him, she will need someone handsome, young, courteous, and entertaining to revive her spirits. Othello has none of these qualities. Lacking the necessary charms in her husband, she will feel poorly matched. She will feel queasy and will loathe and despise the Moor. Natural desires will guide her toward another man. If you agree with my statement, which is truthful and logical, who fits the description of a second man better than Cassio? He's a talkative rascal. Who is more capable of pretending to be mannerly and kind while concealing lust and flirtation? There is no one smoother than he. He is a devious, sneaky rogue. He looks for opportunities to seduce women. He finds chances where there are none. He's a wicked womanizer! Cassio is good-looking, young, and endowed with the qualities that foolish, immature women look for. An all-around skirt-chaser! And Desdemona has already noticed him.

RODERIGO	I can't believe she admires him. She seems high-minded.

IAGO	A fig for high-mindedness! She's human. If she were blessed, she would have rejected Othello. Blessed pudding! Didn't you see her caress Cassio's palm? Didn't you notice?

RODERIGO	Yes, I saw it, but it was only a handshake.

TRANSLATION

IAGO	Lechery, by this hand! an index and obscure 260
	prologue to the history of lust and foul
	thoughts. They met so near with their lips that their
	breaths embraced together. Villainous thoughts,
	Roderigo! When these mutualities so marshal the
	way, hard at hand comes the master and main 265
	exercise, th' incorporate conclusion. Pish! But, sir,
	be you ruled by me: I have brought you from
	Venice. Watch you to-night; for the command, I'll
	lay't upon you. Cassio knows you not. I'll not be far
	from you: do you find some occasion to anger 270
	Cassio, either by speaking too loud, or tainting his
	discipline, or from what other course you please
	which the time shall more favorably minister.
RODERIGO	Well.
IAGO	Sir, he is rash and very sudden in choler, and 275
	haply with his truncheon may strike at you. Provoke
	him that he may; for even out of that will I
	cause these of Cyprus to mutiny; whose qualification
	shall come into no true taste again but the
	displanting of Cassio. So shall you have a shorter 280
	journey to your desires by the means I shall then
	have to prefer them; and the impediment most
	profitably removed without the which there were no
	expectation of our prosperity.
RODERIGO	I will do this if you can bring it to any 285
	opportunity.
IAGO	I warrant thee. Meet me by and by at the
	citadel; I must fetch his necessaries ashore. Farewell.
RODERIGO	Adieu. *[Exit]*

IAGO	Lust, I swear! A beginning and concealed start to desire and dirty thoughts. They came so close together that they breathed each other's breath. Evil thoughts, Roderigo! When such intimacy leads the way, next comes sex, the body's conclusion to lewd fantasies. Pish! Just listen to me. I am the one who brought you from Venice. Join the guard tonight. I'll arrange for your assignment. Cassio doesn't know you. I will be close by. Lure Cassio into a fight, either by being too loud or by belittling his efforts, or by whatever means you choose that suits the situation.

ACT II

RODERIGO	Okay.
IAGO	Cassio is rash and touchy and may even strike you with his nightstick. Bait him into a fight. Then I will turn the squabble into an island riot. The people of Cyprus will accept no solution but the removal of Cassio from the guard. You will gain Desdemona quickly to complete the rest of my plan. I will remove Othello, the only impediment to your romance with Desdemona.
RODERIGO	I will obey you for any opportunity to have her.
IAGO	I promise success. Meet me later at the fort. I have to unload Othello's luggage from the ship. Goodbye.
RODERIGO	God go with you. *[RODERIGO goes out.]*

TRANSLATION

IAGO	That Cassio loves her, I do well believe it;	290
	That she loves him, 'tis apt and of great credit.	
	The Moor, howbeit that I endure him not,	
	Is of a constant, loving, noble nature,	
	And I dare think he'll prove to Desdemona	
	A most dear husband. Now I do love her too;	295
	Not out of absolute lust, though peradventure	
	I stand accountant for as great a sin,	
	But partly led to diet my revenge,	
	For that I do suspect the lusty Moor	
	Hath leaped into my seat; the thought whereof	300
	Doth, like a poisonous mineral, gnaw my inwards;	
	And nothing can or shall content my soul	
	Till I am evened with him, wife for wife:	
	Or failing so, yet that I put the Moor	
	At least into a jealousy so strong	305
	That judgment cannot cure. Which thing to do,	
	If this poor trash of Venice, whom I trash	
	For his quick hunting, stand the putting on,	
	I'll have our Michael Cassio on the hip,	
	Abuse him to the Moor in the rank garb	310
	(For I fear Cassio with my nightcap too),	
	Make the Moor thank me, love me, and reward me	
	For making him egregiously an ass	
	And practicing upon his peace and quiet	
	Even to madness. 'Tis here, but yet confused:	315
	Knavery's plain face is never seen till used.	
	[Exit]	

| IAGO | I believe that Cassio really loves Desdemona. That she will return his affection is likely and possible. Even though I hate Othello, he is a faithful, affectionate, and worthy man. I predict that he will be a loving mate for Desdemona. I love Desdemona, too. Not because I desire her, although I am capable of lusting after women, but because she will further my vengeance. I suspect that Othello has seduced Emilia. The suspicion gnaws at my guts like poison. I won't stop until I rob him of his wife as he stole mine. If I fail, I at least want to make him so jealous that he will never be the same. To accomplish my plot, this Roderigo, a frivolous Venetian, whom I set on the hunt for Cassio, will put Cassio in danger. I will defame Cassio to Othello. (I also fear that Cassio may seduce Emilia.) I will make Othello thank me, like me, and reward me for making a great fool of him. By destroying Othello's peace and contentment, I plan to drive him insane. I have the beginnings of my plot, but I have to work out the details. Deception looks innocent until put into action. *[IAGO goes out.]* |

ACT II

ACT II, SCENE 2

A street.

[Enter OTHELLO's HERALD with a proclamation]

HERALD   It is Othello's pleasure, our noble and valiant
                general, that, upon certain tidings now arrived,
                importing the mere perdition of the Turkish fleet,
                every man put himself into triumph; some to dance,
                some to make bonfires, each man to what sport and   5
                revels his addiction leads him. For, besides these
                beneficial news, it is the celebration of his nuptial.
                So much was his pleasure should be proclaimed. All
                offices are open, and there is full liberty of feasting
                from this present hour of five till the bell have told   10
                eleven. Heaven bless the isle of Cyprus and our
                noble general Othello!
                [Exit]

ACT II, SCENE 2

A street in Cyprus.

[OTHELLO's messenger enters to make an announcement.]

HERALD Our noble, brave General Othello invites all to celebrate the complete destruction of the Turkish navy. Each should choose an entertainment—dancing, bonfires, or whatever enjoyment pleases. It is a double celebration of his victory and his marriage to Desdemona. He wants to share his joy. All establishments will remain open for dinner from 5:00 until the 11:00 p.m. curfew. God bless Cyprus and worthy General Othello! *[The herald goes out.]*

ACT II

TRANSLATION

ACT II, SCENE 3

A hall in the castle.

[Enter OTHELLO, DESDEMONA, CASSIO, and Attendants]

OTHELLO   Good Michael, look you to the guard tonight.
Let's teach ourselves that honorable stop,
Not to outsport discretion.

CASSIO   Iago hath direction what to do;
But not withstanding, with my personal eye   5
Will I look to't.

OTHELLO   Iago is most honest.
Michael, good night. To-morrow with your earliest
Let me have speech with you. *[To DESDEMONA]*
Come, my dear love.
The purchase made, the fruits are to ensue;   10
That profit's yet to come 'tween me and you.
Good night.
[Exit OTHELLO with DESDEMONA and Attendants;
Enter IAGO]

CASSIO   Welcome, Iago. We must to the watch.

IAGO   Not this hour, lieutenant; 'tis not yet ten o'
th' clock. Our general cast us thus early for the love
of his Desdemona; who let us not therefore blame.   15
He hath not yet made wanton the night with her, and
she is sport for Jove.

CASSIO   She's a most exquisite lady.

IAGO   And, I'll warrant her, full of game.

CASSIO   Indeed, she's a most fresh and delicate creature.   20

IAGO   What an eye she has! Methinks it sounds a
parley to provocation.

ACT II, SCENE 3

A hall in the castle.

[OTHELLO, DESDOMONA, CASSIO, and company enter.]

OTHELLO   Cassio, you stand guard tonight. We have to be careful not to let celebration outweigh caution.

CASSIO   Iago knows what to do. I will personally take charge.

OTHELLO   Iago is dependable. Cassio, good night. I want to speak with you early tomorrow morning. *[To DESDEMONA]* Come, sweetheart. The battle won, we deserve some fun. Later, we will make love. Good night. *[OTHELLO departs with DESDEMONA and company; IAGO enters.]*

CASSIO   Greetings, Iago. We must stand guard.

IAGO   Not until 10:00 p.m., lieutenant. General Othello dismissed us early so he can spend time with Desdemona. He has not yet spent a night with her. She is worthy of the god Jupiter.

CASSIO   She is a gorgeous woman.

IAGO   And, I'll bet, very sexy.

CASSIO   Yes, she is both youthful and refined.

IAGO   She has flirty eyes! I think she provokes men.

CASSIO	An inviting eye; and yet methinks right modest.
IAGO	And when she speaks, is it not an alarum to love?
CASSIO	She is indeed perfection. 25
IAGO	Well, happiness to their sheets! Come, lieutenant, I have a stoup of wine, and here without are a brace of Cyprus gallants that would fain have a measure to the health of black Othello.
CASSIO	Not to-night, good Iago. I have very poor 30 and unhappy brains for drinking; I could well wish courtesy would invent some other custom of entertainment.
IAGO	O, they are our friends. But one cup! I'll drink for you. 35
CASSIO	I have drunk but one cup to-night, and that was craftily qualified too; and behold what innovation it makes here. I am unfortunate in the infirmity and dare not task my weakness with any more.
IAGO	What, man! 'Tis a night of revels: the gallants 40 desire it.
CASSIO	Where are they?
IAGO	Here at the door; I pray you call them in.
CASSIO	I'll do't, but it dislikes me. *[Exit]*

CASSIO	She is seductive, but I think she is modest.
IAGO	And her words, don't they invite romance?
CASSIO	She is truly the perfect woman.
IAGO	I wish them joy of their bed! Come with me, Lieutenant Cassio, I have a pitcher of wine. All about us are Cyprus patriots who want to drink to Othello's health.
CASSIO	I can't drink tonight, Iago. I get drunk too easily. I wish people would invent another form of amusement.
IAGO	We are among friends. Let's have one cup of wine! I'll drink the toasts for you.
CASSIO	I have drunk only one glass of wine tonight, which I carefully diluted with water. Look how it muddles my thinking. I am a poor drinker. I don't dare tempt my weakness any further.
IAGO	What, Cassio! This is a celebration. The patriots encourage it.
CASSIO	Where are they?
IAGO	They wait at the door. Invite them in.
CASSIO	I will invite them, but I'd rather not. *[CASSIO goes out.]*

ACT II

TRANSLATION

IAGO	If I can fasten but one cup upon him	45
	With that which he hath drunk to-night already,	
	He'll be as full of quarrel and offense	
	As my young mistress' dog. Now my sick fool Roderigo,	
	Whom love hath turned almost the wrong side out,	
	To Desdemona hath to-night caroused	50
	Potations pottle-deep; and he's to watch.	
	Three lads of Cyprus—Noble swelling spirits,	
	That hold their honors in a wary distance,	
	The very elements of this warlike isle—	
	Have I to-night flustered with flowing cups,	55
	And they watch too. Now, 'mongst this flock of drunkards	
	Am I to put our Cassio in some action	
	That may offend the isle.	

[Enter CASSIO, MONTANO, and Gentlemen; Servants following with wine]

	But here they come.	
	If consequence do but approve my dream,	
	My boat sails freely, both with wind and stream.	60

| CASSIO | 'Fore God, they have given me a rouse already. | |

| MONTANO | Good faith, a little one; not past a pint, as I am a soldier. | |

IAGO	Some wine, ho!	65
	[Sings] And let me the canakin clink, clink;	
	And let me the canakin clink.	
	A soldier's a man;	
	A life's but a span,	
	Why then, let a soldier drink.	70
	Some wine, boys!	

| CASSIO | 'Fore God, an excellent song! | |

| IAGO | I learned it in England, where indeed they are most potent in potting. Your Dane, your German, and your swag-bellied Hollander—Drink, ho!— are nothing to your English. | 75 |

| CASSIO | Is your Englishman so expert in his drinking? | |

| IAGO | If I can get one more glass of wine in him, added to the cup he has already drunk, he will become as feisty and quarrelsome as Desdemona's dog. In addition, Roderigo, the lovesick idiot, is so addle-headed that he has drunk two-quart tankards to the bottom. I have to keep an eye on Roderigo. I have already caroused with three young men from Cyprus, noble boys who bristle at a chance to defend the island's reputation for war. All three stand watch. Now I will place Cassio in the ranks of the three drunken men and nudge him into insulting Cyprus. *[CASSIO, MONTANO, and gentlemen enter. Servants bring in more wine.]* Here they are. If the situation suits my plan, I will sail downstream with the wind. |

ACT II

| CASSIO | I swear, they have already poured me a drink. |

| MONTANO | I promise, it's a small one; no more than two cups, I declare as a soldier. |

| IAGO | Bring wine here! *[IAGO sings]* And let me clink glasses. A soldier is only mortal. Life is short. Then, let soldiers drink. Have some wine, boys! |

| CASSIO | By God, that was an excellent drinking song! |

| IAGO | I learned it in England, where people like to drink. The Danish, the Germans, and the big-gutted Dutch—everybody drink up—don't compare to the English for drinking. |

| CASSIO | Are the English as good at holding their drink? |

TRANSLATION

| IAGO | Why, he drinks you with facility your Dane dead drunk; he sweats not to overthrow your Almain; he gives your Hollander a vomit ere the next pottle can be filled. | 80 |

CASSIO   To the health of our general!

MONTANO   I am for it, lieutenant, and I'll do you justice.

IAGO   O sweet England!
[Sings] King Stephen was a worthy peer;   85
His breeches cost him but a crown;
He held 'em sixpence all too dear,
With that he called the tailor lown.
He was a wight of high renown,
And thou art but of low degree.   90
'Tis pride that pulls the country down;
Then take thine auld cloak about thee.
Some wine, ho!

CASSIO   'Fore God, this is a more exquisite song
than the other.   95

IAGO   Will you hear't again?

CASSIO   No, for I hold him to be unworthy of his
place that does those things. Well, God's above all;
and there be souls must be saved, and there be souls
must not be saved.   100

IAGO   It's true, good lieutenant.

CASSIO   For mine own part—no offense to the
general, nor any man of quality—I hope to be saved.

IAGO   And so do I too, lieutenant.

CASSIO   Ay, but, by your leave, not before me. The   105
lieutenant is to be saved before the ancient. Let's
have no more of this; let's to our affairs.—God
forgive us our sins!—Gentlemen, let's look to our
business. Do not think, gentlemen, I am drunk. This
is my ancient; this is my right hand, and this is my   110
left. I am not drunk now. I can stand well enough,
and speak well enough.

ALL   Excellent well!

ORIGINAL

IAGO	The English drink the Danes under the table. The English boozer doesn't worry about outdrinking the German. The Dutch is already vomiting before he can refill the two-quart tankard.
CASSIO	To the health of General Othello!
MONTANO	I will join you, Lieutenant Cassio, and I'll match you glass for glass.
IAGO	Oh, wonderful England! *[IAGO sings]* King Stephen was an honorable noble. He paid only five dollars for his pants. He called the tailor a lout for overcharging him six cents. Stephen was well respected and you are only a peasant. Pride in wardrobe weakens England. Wrap yourself in an old coat, then. Bring more wine!
CASSIO	By God, that is a better drinking song than the first one.
IAGO	Shall I sing it again?
CASSIO	No. Repeating the song would cheapen you. Well, God rules us. Some souls must be rescued and some not.
IAGO	That's true, Lieutenant Cassio.
CASSIO	As for myself—no dishonor to General Othello or to any other respectable man—I hope I will be saved.
IAGO	And I also hope to be saved, Lieutenant.
CASSIO	Yes, but not before I am saved. A lieutenant outranks a flag bearer. Let's talk about something else. Let's get to work. God forgive us our faults!—Gentlemen, let's depart for guard duty. Don't assume, gentlemen, that I am too drunk for duty. This is my flag bearer. This is my right hand and this is my left hand. I'm not drunk. I can stand up and speak sense.
ALL	And very well.

ACT II

TRANSLATION

CASSIO	Why, very well then. You must not think
	then that I am drunk. 115
	[Exit]
MONTANO	To th' platform, masters. Come, let's set the watch.
IAGO	You see this fellow that is gone before.
	He is a soldier fit to stand by Caesar
	And give direction; and do but see his vice.
	'Tis to his virtue a just equinox, 120
	The one as long as th' other. 'Tis pity of him.
	I fear the trust Othello puts him in,
	On some odd time of his infirmity,
	Will shake this island.
MONTANO	But is he often thus?
IAGO	'Tis evermore the prologue to his sleep: 125
	He'll watch the horologe a double set
	If drink rock not his cradle.
MONTANO	It were well
	The general were put in mind of it.
	Perhaps he sees it not, or his good nature
	Prizes the virtue that appears in Cassio 130
	And looks not on his evils. Is not this true?
	[Enter RODERIGO]
IAGO	*[Aside to him]* How now, Roderigo?
	I pray you after the lieutenant, go!
	[Exit RODERIGO]
MONTANO	And 'tis great pity that the noble Moor
	Should hazard such a place as his own second 135
	With one of an ingraft infirmity.
	It were an honest action to say
	So to the Moor.
IAGO	Not I, for this fair island!
	I do love Cassio well and would do much
	To cure him of this evil. *[Within]* Help! help!
	But hark! What noise? 140
	[Enter CASSIO, driving in RODERIGO]
CASSIO	Zounds, you rogue! you rascal!
MONTANO	What's the matter, lieutenant?

CASSIO	Okay, then. Don't assume that I am drunk. *[He goes out.]*
MONTANO	To the watchtower, men. Come on, let's begin our watch.
IAGO	You see this man who leads us. He is a soldier worthy to guard Caesar and give orders. And also notice that he has a weakness. He is equally good and weak. It's a pity. I am afraid that Othello's trust in Cassio will threaten island security some time when Cassio is drunk.
MONTANO	Does he get drunk often?
IAGO	He drinks to help him sleep. Without a bedtime drink, he will stay awake twenty-four hours.
MONTANO	Someone needs to warn General Othello of Cassio's weakness. Perhaps Othello hasn't witnessed Cassio's drinking. Or perhaps Othello values Cassio's assets too much to examine his weakness. Isn't this possible? *[RODERIGO enters.]*
IAGO	*[In private to RODERIGO]* What's happening, Roderigo? Please follow Lieutenant Cassio. Go! *[RODERIGO goes out.]*
MONTANO	It is a shame that the noble general risks having a second-in-command who has an innate lust for drink. It is a good reason for alerting Othello.
IAGO	I wouldn't tell Othello, not for the whole island of Cyprus! I like Cassio and would do anything to cure him of drunkenness. *[From the castle]* Help, help! Listen! What was that cry? *[CASSIO enters, pushing RODERIGO in front of him.]*
CASSIO	God's wounds, you villain! you scamp!
MONTANO	What's the matter, lieutenant?

ACT II

CASSIO   A knave teach me my duty?
I'll beat the knave into a twiggen bottle.

RODERIGO   Beat me?

CASSIO   Dost thou prate, rogue?
[Strikes him]

MONTANO   Nay, good lieutenant!
[Stays him]
Pray, sir, hold your hand.   145

CASSIO   Let me go, sir,
Or I'll knock you o'er the mazzard.

MONTANO   Come, come, you're
drunk!

CASSIO   Drunk?
[They fight.]

IAGO   *[Aside to RODERIGO]* Away, I say! Go out and cry a mutiny!
[Exit RODERIGO]
Nay, good lieutenant. God's will, gentlemen!
Help, ho!—lieutenant—sir—Montano—sir—   150
Help, masters!—Here's a goodly watch indeed!
[A bell rung]
Who's that which rings the bell? Diablo, ho!
The town will rise. God's will, lieutenant, hold!
You will be shamed for ever.
[Enter OTHELLO and Gentlemen with weapons]

OTHELLO   What is the matter here?

MONTANO   Zounds, I bleed still. I am hurt to the death.   155
He dies!

OTHELLO   Hold for your lives!

IAGO   Hold, hold! Lieutenant—sir—Montano—gentlemen!
Have you forgot all sense of place and duty?
Hold! The general speaks to you. Hold, hold, for shame!   160

CASSIO	An underling criticizing my performance of duty? I'll beat the rascal until he crawls into a wicker-covered wine bottle.
RODERIGO	You would strike me?
CASSIO	Do you talk back, rascal? *[CASSIO hits RODERIGO.]*
MONTANO	Stop, Cassio! *[MONTANO stops CASSIO from hitting RODERIGO.]* Please, don't hit him.
CASSIO	Let go of me, Montano, or I'll smack you over the head.
MONTANO	Please stop. You're drunk!
CASSIO	Drunk? *[CASSIO and MONTANO fight.]*
IAGO	*[In private to RODERIGO]* Hurry, I tell you. Go and yell "riot"! *[RODERIGO goes out.]* Stop, Cassio. By God, you two! Help me—Cassio—sir—Montano—sir. Help, officers! This is a poor excuse for a security guard! *[An alarm bell rings.]* Who has rung the alarm? Oh, the devil! That bell will waken the town. By God, Cassio, stop! Your behavior will bring eternal shame on you. *[OTHELLO and gentlemen enter with weapons.]*
OTHELLO	What is happening here?
MONTANO	God's wounds, I am bleeding. I am mortally wounded. Cassio will die for it!
OTHELLO	Stop or I kill you both!
IAGO	Stop, stop! Cassio—sir—Montano—gentlemen! Have you forgotten your rank and duty? Stop! Othello is addressing you. Stop, stop, shame on you!

ACT II

OTHELLO	Why, how now, ho? From whence ariseth this?
	Are we turned Turks, and to ourselves do that
	Which heaven hath forbid the Ottomites?
	For Christian shame put by this barbarous brawl!
	He that stirs next to carve for his own rage

165

Holds his soul light; he dies upon his motion.
Silence that dreadful bell! It frights the isle
From her propriety. What's the matter, masters?
Honest Iago, that looks dead with grieving,
Speak. Who began this? On thy love, I charge thee.

170

IAGO
I do not know. Friends all but now, even now,
In quarter, and in terms like bride and groom
Devesting them for bed; and then, but now—
As if some planet had unwitted men—
Swords out, and tilting one at other's breast

175

In opposition bloody. I cannot speak
Any beginning to this peevish odds,
And would in action glorious I had lost
Those legs that brought me to a part of it!

OTHELLO
How comes it, Michael, you are thus forgot?

180

CASSIO
I pray you pardon me; I cannot speak.

OTHELLO
Worthy Montano, you were wont be civil;
The gravity and stillness of your youth
The world hath noted, and your name is great
In mouths of wisest censure. What's the matter

185

That you unlace your reputation thus
And spend your rich opinion for the name
Of a night-brawler? Give me answer to't.

MONTANO
Worthy Othello, I am hurt to danger.
Your officer, Iago, can inform you,

190

While I spare speech, which something now offends me,
Of all that I do know; nor know I aught
By me that's said or done amiss this night,
Unless self-charity be sometimes a vice,
And to defend ourselves it be a sin

195

When violence assails us.

OTHELLO   What is happening? What caused this fight? Are we turn-
ing into Turks and fighting our own men? Christians
shame themselves by such street brawling! The next man
who turns anger into fight risks death. He will die on the
spot. Stop ringing that cursed alarm! It scares islanders
into uproar. What is the cause of this duel, gentlemen?
Good Iago, you look as sorrowful as death. Tell me. Who
started this fight? On your friendship, I demand an
explanation.

IAGO   I don't know. One minute they were friendly and under
control like a wedded couple undressing for bed. The
next minute—as if some heavenly power drove them
insane—they drew swords and went at each other like
bloodthirsty enemies. I don't know what started this silly
tussle. I wish I had lost in battle the legs that carried me
to this scene!

OTHELLO   What is wrong with you, Cassio, that you forget your
duty?

CASSIO   Please excuse me. I can't say.

OTHELLO   Montano, you are usually polite. People admire your
maturity and seriousness. You have a good reputation
among the wise. How can you risk your good name in so
trivial a fight? How can you waste your respectability by
brawling by night in public? Answer me.

MONTANO   Worthy Othello, I am seriously wounded. Iago, your flag
bearer, can fill in the details. I can't talk because pain
stops me from explaining the situation. I have done or
said nothing wrong tonight. Unless self-defense is wrong
or unless it is a crime to ward off an attacker.

TRANSLATION

OTHELLO   Now, by heaven,
My blood begins my safer guides to rule,
And passion, having my best judgment collied,
Assays to lead the way. If I once stir
Or do but lift this arm, the best of you   200
Shall sink in my rebuke. Give me to know
How this foul rout began, who set it on;
And he that is approved in this offense,
Though he had twinned with me, both at a birth,
Shall lose me. What! in a town of war,   205
Yet wild, the people's hearts brimful of fear,
To manage private and domestic quarrel?
In night, and on the court and guard of safety?
'Tis monstrous. Iago, who began't?

MONTANO If partially affined, or leagued in office,   210
Thou dost deliver more or less than truth,
Thou art no soldier.

IAGO   Touch me not so near.
I had rather have this tongue cut from my mouth
Than it should do offense to Michael Cassio;
Yet I persuade myself, to speak the truth   215
Shall nothing wrong him. Thus it is, general.
Montano and myself being in speech,
There comes a fellow crying out for help,
And Cassio following him with determined sword
To execute upon him. Sir, this gentleman   220
Steps in to Cassio and entreats his pause.
Myself the crying fellow did pursue,
Lest by his clamor—as it so fell out
The town might fall in fright. He, swift of foot,
Outran my purpose; and I returned the rather   225
For that I heard the clink and fall of swords,
And Cassio high in oath; which till to-night
I ne'er might say before. When I came back—
For this was brief—I found them close together
At blow and thrust, even as again they were   230
When you yourself did part them.
More of this matter cannot I report;
But men are men; the best sometimes forget.
Though Cassio did some little wrong to him,
As men in rage strike those that wish them best,   235
Yet surely Cassio I believe received
From him that fled some strange indignity,
Which patience could not pass.

OTHELLO	By God, my outrage overwhelms good sense. Anger, which soils my good judgment, tries to rule me. If I raise my fist, one of you will fall from the blow. Tell me immediately how this brawl began, who started it. Whoever is the guilty party, even if he were my twin brother, shall lose my admiration. How can you provoke a fight in a town still recovering from war? How can you terrorize these nervous citizens with a private, personal spat? How can you fight in the night while you are supposed to be on guard duty? This is an outrage. Iago, who started it?
MONTANO	If you are swayed by friendship or comradeship and tell a half-truth, you violate military principles.
IAGO	Don't presume to know my feelings. I would rather lose my tongue than to slander Michael Cassio. I believe that the truth will not hurt him. This is what happened, General Othello. While I was talking to Montano, a man approached yelling for help. Cassio followed the man and drew his sword to settle the matter. Othello, Montano pursued Cassio and ordered him to stop. I followed the citizen calling for help to stop his yelling—as a result, just as I feared, the whole town jolted awake. The citizen was so fast that he outran me. I came back because I heard the clash of swords. I found Cassio, a sworn officer, doing what I had never seen before. When I arrived—this happened quickly—I discovered Cassio and Montano engaged in a sword fight. They clashed a second time, when you pulled them apart. I don't know any other details. Men are only human; the best sometimes fall into bad behavior. Even though Cassio may have harmed Montano, as angry men strike even friends, I am certain that Cassio suffered some unforeseen insult that he could not forgive.

ACT II

TRANSLATION

OTHELLO   I know, Iago,
Thy honesty and love doth mince this matter,
Making it light to Cassio. Cassio, I love thee;   240
But never more be officer of mine.
[Enter DESDEMONA, attended]
Look if my gentle love be not raised up!
I'll make thee an example.

DESDEMONA   What's the matter?

OTHELLO   All's well now, sweeting; come away to bed.
[To MONTANO] Sir, for your hurts, myself will be your
    surgeon.   245
Lead him off. *[MONTANO is led off.]*
Iago, look with care about the town
And silence those whom this vile brawl distracted.
Come, Desdemona: 'tis the soldiers' life
To have their balmy slumbers waked with strife.   250
[Exeunt with all but IAGO and CASSIO]

IAGO   What, are you hurt, lieutenant?

CASSIO   Ay, past all surgery.

IAGO   Marry, God forbid!

CASSIO   Reputation, reputation, reputation! O, I
have lost my reputation! I have lost the immortal   255
part of myself, and what remains is bestial. My
reputation, Iago, my reputation!

IAGO   As I am an honest man, I thought you had
received some bodily wound. There is more sense
in that than in reputation. Reputation is an idle   260
and most false imposition; oft got without merit and
lost without deserving. You have lost no reputation
at all unless you repute yourself such a loser. What,
man! there are ways to recover the general again.
You are but now cast in his mood—a punishment   265
more in policy than in malice, even so as one
would beat his offenseless dog to affright an
imperious lion. Sue to him again, and he's yours.

OTHELLO	I am aware, Iago, that your sincerity and admiration weaken the truth to help Cassio. Cassio, you are my friend, but you can never serve on my staff. *[DESDEMONA enters with a lady-in-waiting.]* You have awakened my sweet wife! I will make an example of you, Cassio.
DESDEMONA	What is happening?
OTHELLO	All is settled, sweetheart. Go back to bed. *[To MONTANO]* Sir, I will treat your wounds myself. Take him away. *[MONTANO is helped offstage.]* Iago, patrol the town and quiet anyone whom this duel disturbed. Come with me, Desdemona. It is not unusual for professional soldiers to be awakened from sleep by fighting. *[All depart except IAGO and CASSIO.]*
IAGO	Are you wounded, Cassio?
CASSIO	Yes, more than medicine can cure.
IAGO	Really? Heaven forbid!
CASSIO	My reputation is ruined! The best part of me is lost. All that is left is a beast. My reputation, Iago. I have lost respect!
IAGO	Truly, I thought you had a sword wound. There is more pain from a sword thrust than from disrespect. Fame is a faulty award requiring no effort from the receiver. People often earn respect without deserving it and lose respect through no fault of their own. You have lost no prestige unless you think of yourself as disreputable. Think, Cassio! There are ways to regain Othello's trust. You caught him at a bad moment. He punishes you more out of military duty than from hatred. He lashes out at you like a man beating a helpless dog to terrify a lion. Ask him later and he will reinstate you.

ACT II

TRANSLATION

| CASSIO | I will rather sue to be despised than to deceive so good a commander with so slight, so drunken, and so indiscreet an officer. Drunk! And speak parrot! and squabble! swagger! swear! and discourse fustian with one's own shadow! O thou invisible spirit of wine, if thou hast no name to be known by, let us call thee devil! | 270 |
| | | 275 |

| IAGO | What was he that you followed with your sword? What had he done to you? | |

| CASSIO | I know not. | |

| IAGO | Is't possible? | |

| CASSIO | I remember a mass of things, but nothing distinctly; a quarrel, but nothing wherefore. O God, that men should put an enemy in their mouths to steal away their brains! that we should with joy, pleasance, revel and applause transform ourselves into beasts! | 280 |
| | | 285 |

| IAGO | Why, but you are now well enough. How came you thus recovered? | |

| CASSIO | It hath pleased the devil drunkenness to give place to the devil wrath. One unperfectness shows me another, to make me frankly despise myself. | 290 |

| IAGO | Come, you are too severe a moraler. As the time, the place, and the condition of this country stands, I could heartily wish this had not so befall'n; but since it is as it is, mend it for your own good. | 295 |

| CASSIO | I will ask him for my place again: he shall tell me I am a drunkard! Had I as many mouths as Hydra, such an answer would stop them all. To be now a sensible man, by and by a fool, and presently a beast! O strange! Every inordinate cup is unblest, and the ingredient is a devil. | 300 |

CASSIO	I would rather beg him to hate me rather than to lie to my worthy commander about so petty, so drunk, and so rash an officer. Drunk! And babbling! and squabbling! strutting! swearing! and spouting gibberish to my shadow! Oh, intoxication, if you have no other name, you should be called a demon!
IAGO	Why did Montano raise his sword against you? What caused his anger?
CASSIO	I don't know.
IAGO	Why don't you know?
CASSIO	I remember a blur, but no details. I remember the quarrel, but not the cause. Oh, God, why do men pour dangerous wine into their mouths and let it destroy their reason! Why do we gladly, for pleasure, celebration, and approval turn ourselves into animals!
IAGO	You seem sober now. How did you sober up so fast?
CASSIO	The demon of drink changed places with the demon of anger. One weakness unleashes another weakness to make me hate myself.
IAGO	Don't be so hard on yourself. Because of the recent war off the island of Cyprus, I wish that this quarrel had not occurred. Because it has happened, you must smooth over the situation for your own good.
CASSIO	If I ask to be reinstated as lieutenant, Othello will call me a drunk! If I had as many mouths as the hundred-headed Hydra, his charge would shut them up. I went from sane man to fool to an animal. It seems odd! The more I drink, the more I damn myself with devilish intoxication.

ACT II

TRANSLATION

IAGO	Come, come, good wine is a good familiar creature if it be well used. Exclaim no more against it. And, good lieutenant, I think you think I love you. 305
CASSIO	I have well approved it, sir. I drunk!
IAGO	You or any man living may be drunk at some time, man. I'll tell you what you shall do. Our general's wife is now the general. I may say so in this respect, for that he hath devoted and given up himself to the 310 contemplation, mark, and denotement of her parts and graces. Confess yourself freely to her; importune her help to put you in your place again. She is of so free, so kind, so apt, so blessed a disposition she holds it a vice in her goodness not to do more than 315 she is requested. This broken joint between you and her husband entreat her to splinter; and my fortunes against any lay worth naming, this crack of your love shall grow stronger than 'twas before. 320
CASSIO	You advise me well.
IAGO	I protest, in the sincerity of love and honest kindness.
CASSIO	I think it freely; and betimes in the morning will I beseech the virtuous Desdemona to undertake for me. I am desperate of my fortunes if they 325 check me here.
IAGO	You are in the right. Good night, lieutenant; I must to the watch.
CASSIO	Good night, honest Iago. *[Exit CASSIO]*

IAGO	Don't exaggerate. Good wine is a friend if you control your drinking. Don't condemn wine. And, Cassio, you know I'm your friend.
CASSIO	I have proof of your friendship. Me! A drunk!
IAGO	Anybody can drink too much. I have a suggestion. Desdemona controls Othello. By this I mean that he has so absorbed himself in her physical beauty and grace. Tell her your story and beg her to speak to Othello on your behalf. She has so generous, kind, willing, and good a nature that she blames herself for not doing more for people. She can heal this break between you and Othello. I am willing to bet that your relationship with Othello will be even stronger than before.

ACT II

CASSIO	You give good advice.
IAGO	I speak out of friendship and sincere kindness.
CASSIO	I will think it over. Tomorrow morning, I will beg the good-hearted Desdemona to help me. My career is ruined if I lose my military rank.
IAGO	You are right about that. Good night, Cassio. I must return to guard duty.
CASSIO	Good night, friend Iago. *[CASSIO goes out.]*

TRANSLATION

IAGO	And what's he then that says I play the villain,	330
	When this advice is free I give and honest,	
	Probal to thinking, and indeed the course	
	To win the Moor again? For 'tis most easy	
	Th' inclining Desdemona to subdue	
	In any honest suit; she's framed as fruitful	335
	As the free elements. And then for her	
	To win the Moor—were't to renounce his baptism,	
	All seals and symbols of redeemed sin—	
	His soul is so enfettered to her love	
	That she may make, unmake, do what she list,	340
	Even as her appetite shall play the god	
	With his weak function. How am I then a villain	
	To counsel Cassio to this parallel course,	
	Directly to his good? Divinity of hell!	
	When devils will the blackest sins put on,	345
	They do suggest at first with heavenly shows,	
	As I do now. For whiles this honest fool	
	Plies Desdemona to repair his fortunes,	
	And she for him pleads strongly to the Moor,	
	I'll pour this pestilence into his ear,	350
	That she repeals him for her body's lust;	
	And by how much she strives to do him good,	
	She shall undo her credit with the Moor.	
	So will I turn her virtue into pitch,	
	And out of her own goodness make the net	355
	That shall enmesh them all.	
	[Enter RODERIGO]	
	How, now Roderigo?	

RODERIGO	I do follow here in the chase, not like a hound	
	that hunts, but one that fills up the cry. My money	
	is almost spent; I have been to-night exceedingly	
	well cudgelled; and I think the issue will be—	360
	I shall have so much experience for my pains;	
	and so, with no money at all, and a little more wit,	
	return again to Venice.	

IAGO   Who can say that I am criminal. I gave Cassio free and sincere advice. Isn't it reasonable and sensible to persuade Othello to forgive Cassio? It is easy to beg the helpful Desdemona to take sides with any honest mistake. She is known for being as generous as earth, air, fire, and water. She can easily persuade Othello, even to giving up his religion and his salvation. Her love binds his soul so tightly that she can do anything she wants with it. Her desires reign over his need for her. Why does my advice to Cassio make me a criminal? My goodness is really Hellish! The most sinful devils cover themselves in righteousness as I have done. While this innocent Cassio begs Desdemona to restore his good name and while she pleads on his behalf to Othello, I will poison Othello's trust by implying that Desdemona defends Cassio because of her sexual desire for Cassio. While she tries to help Cassio, she will be discrediting herself with Othello. Thus, I will twist her goodness into blackness. Out of her kindness, I will weave a net to capture Desdemona, Othello, and Cassio. *[RODERIGO enters.]* What is it, Roderigo?

RODERIGO   I am pursuing Desdemona, not like a successful hunting hound, but like one that cries from a dog pack. I have spent most of my money. Tonight, I have been thoroughly outwitted. Out of this experience, I have gained little. I will go home to Venice broke and outsmarted.

TRANSLATION

IAGO	How poor are they that have not patience!	
	What wound did ever heal but by degrees!	365
	Thou know'st we work by wit, and not by witchcraft;	
	And wit depends on dilatory time.	
	Does't not go well? Cassio hath beaten thee,	
	And thou by that small hurt hast cashiered Cassio.	
	Though other things grow fair against the sun,	370
	Yet fruits that blossom first will first be ripe.	
	Content thyself awhile. By the mass, 'tis morning!	
	Pleasure and action make the hours seem short.	
	Retire thee; go where thou art billeted.	
	Away, I say! Thou shalt know more hereafter.	375
	Nay, get thee gone!	
	[Exit RODERIGO]	
	Two things are to be done:	
	My wife must move for Cassio to her mistress;	
	I'll set her on;	
	Myself the while to draw the Moor apart	
	And bring him jump when he may Cassio find	380
	Soliciting his wife. Ay, that's the way!	
	Dull not device by coldness and delay.	
	[Exit]	

IAGO   Be patient! You can repair the damage a bit at a time! Because we use our heads rather than magic, we must be prepared to move slowly. Aren't we advancing toward our goal? Cassio struck you and you, with little effort, ruined Cassio. Though other issues progress, our aim must advance from blossom to ripeness. Be patient. By the holy mass, it is already morning! Hours fly by when we enjoy our actions. Go to your assigned bed. Go on! You will learn more later. Don't argue. Go! *[RODERIGO goes out.]* I have two things to accomplish. Emilia must plead Cassio's case to Desdemona. I will inform Emilia. Meanwhile, I must guide Othello at just the right moment to watch Cassio begging Desdemona for help. Yes, that's my plan! Don't ruin it by lack of energy and time-wasting. *[He goes out.]*

ACT II

TRANSLATION

ACT III, SCENE 1

Before the castle.

[Enter CASSIO with Musicians]

CASSIO	Masters, play here, I will content your pains:
	Something that's brief; and bid 'Good morrow, general.'
	[Music]
	[Enter the Clown]
CLOWN	Why, masters, ha' your instruments been at
	Naples, that they speak i' th' nose thus?
MUSICIAN	How, sir, how?
CLOWN	Are these, I pray, called wind instruments?
MUSICIAN	Ay, marry, are they, sir.
CLOWN	O, thereby hangs a tail.
MUSICIAN	Whereby hangs a tale, sir?
CLOWN	Marry, sir, by many a wind instrument that
	I know. But, masters, here's money for you. And the
	general so likes your music that he desires you, for
	love's sake, to make no more noise with it.
MUSICIAN	Well, sir, we will not.
CLOWN	If you have any music that may not be heard,
	to't again: but, as they say, to hear music the
	general does not greatly care.
MUSICIAN	We have none such, sir.
CLOWN	Then put up your pipes in your bag, for I'll
	away. Go vanish into air, away!
	[Exit Musician with his fellows]
CASSIO	Dost thou hear, my honest friend?
CLOWN	No, I hear not your honest friend. I hear you.
CASSIO	Prithee keep up thy quillets. There's a poor piece
	of gold for thee. If the gentlewoman that attends
	the general's wife be stirring, tell her there's one
	Cassio entreats her a little favor of speech. Wilt
	thou do this?

Line numbers: 5, 10, 15, 20, 25

ACT III, SCENE 1

In front of the castle on the island of Cyprus.

[CASSIO enters with musicians.]

CASSIO Players, perform here. I will pay you. Choose something short and say, "Good morning, General Othello." *[Music sounds.] [A clown enters.]*

CLOWN Players, have your musical instruments been to Naples? They sound nasal.

MUSICIAN What was that, sir?

CLOWN Are these wind instruments?

MUSICIAN Indeed they are, sir.

CLOWN There hangs a tail.

MUSICIAN Where is the tale, sir?

CLOWN By many wind instruments that I have seen. Players, here is your pay. Othello likes your playing so well that he asks you to stop.

MUSICIAN Well, we won't.

CLOWN If you have any silent music, play it. The general is not fond of music.

MUSICIAN We have no silent music, sir.

CLOWN Then put your instruments in their cases. I am leaving. Go away! Disappear! *[The musician departs with the other players.]*

CASSIO Are you listening, my good friend?

CLOWN I don't hear your friend. I hear you.

CASSIO Please continue making plays on words. Here's a small gold coin for you. If the lady-in-waiting to Othello's wife is awake, tell her that Cassio would like to speak with her. Will you do what I ask?

ACT III

CLOWN	She is stirring, sir. If she will stir hither, I shall seem to notify unto her.
CASSIO	Do, good my friend. *[Exit Clown] [Enter IAGO]* 30 In happy time, Iago.
IAGO	You have not been abed then?
CASSIO	Why, no; the day had broke Before we parted. I have made bold, Iago, To send in to your wife: my suit to her Is that she will to virtuous Desdemona 35 Procure me some access.
IAGO	I'll send her to you presently; And I'll devise a mean to draw the Moor Out of the way, that your converse and business May be more free.
CASSIO	I humbly thank you for't. *[Exit IAGO]* 40 I never knew A Florentine more kind and honest. *[Enter EMILIA]*
EMILIA	Good morrow, good lieutenant. I am sorry For your displeasure; but all will sure be well. The general and his wife are talking of it, 45 And she speaks for you stoutly. The Moor replies That he you hurt is of great fame in Cyprus And great affinity, and that in wholesome wisdom He might not but refuse you; but he protests he loves you, And needs no other suitor but his likings 50 To take the safest occasion by the front To bring you in again.
CASSIO	Yet I beseech you, If you think fit, or that it may be done, Give me advantage of some brief discourse With Desdemona alone. 55
EMILIA	Pray you come in. I will bestow you where you shall have time To speak your bosom freely.
CASSIO	I am much bound to you. *[Exeunt]*

CLOWN	She is awake. If she comes outdoors, I will give her your message.
CASSIO	Do it, good friend. *[The clown goes out.] [IAGO enters.]* A fortunate meeting, Iago.
IAGO	Haven't you been to bed at all?
CASSIO	No. Day dawned before I left you. I have dared to send for your wife, Iago. I will ask her to seek an audience for me with Desdemona.
IAGO	I will send Emilia to you immediately. I will pull Othello aside so you may conduct your business in private.
CASSIO	I humbly thank you. *[IAGO goes out.]* I never knew a kinder, more honest person from Florence. *[EMILIA enters.]*
EMILIA	Good morning, Lieutenant Cassio. I am sorry about your loss of promotion. Everything will work out. Othello and Desdemona are discussing your situation. She is on your side. Othello declares that Montano, whom you struck, is respected and well connected in Cyprus. To settle the situation, Othello felt it wise to charge you. He says that he is fond of you. He requires no other begging to reinstate you at a favorable time.
CASSIO	I beg you, if you think it polite and if you think it is possible, to let me talk alone with Desdemona.
EMILIA	Please come in. I will escort you to a place where you may speak privately with her.
CASSIO	I am obliged to you. *[EMILIA and CASSIO go out.]*

ACT III

TRANSLATION

ACT III, SCENE 2

A room in the castle.

[Enter OTHELLO, IAGO, and Gentlemen]

OTHELLO   These letters give, Iago, to the pilot
And by him do my duties to the Senate.
That done, I will be walking on the works;
Repair there to me.

IAGO   Well, my good lord, I'll do't.

OTHELLO   This fortification, gentlemen, shall we see't?   5

GENTLEMEN We'll wait upon your lordship.
[Exeunt]

ACT III, SCENE 2

A room in the castle on Cyprus.

[OTHELLO, IAGO, and gentlemen enter.]

OTHELLO   Convey these letter to the navigator, Iago, to complete my duty to the Senate in Venice. When you finish, join me for a walk on the fortress walls.

IAGO   Yes, my lord, I will.

OTHELLO   Gentlemen, shall we inspect the fort?

GENTLEMEN   We will accompany you. *[They go out.]*

ACT III, SCENE 3

The garden of the castle.

[Enter DESDEMONA, CASSIO, and EMILIA]

DESDEMONA	Be thou assured, good Cassio, I will do All my abilities in thy behalf.
EMILIA	Good madam, do. I warrant it grieves my husband As if the cause were his.
DESDEMONA	O, that's an honest fellow. Do not doubt, Cassio, 5 But I will have my lord and you again As friendly as you were.
CASSIO	Bounteous madam, Whatever shall become of Michael Cassio, He's never anything but your true servant.
DESDEMONA	I know't; I thank you. You do love my lord; 10 You have known him long; and be you well assured He shall in strangeness stand no farther off Than in a politic distance.
CASSIO	Ay, but, lady, That policy may either last so long, Or feed upon such nice and waterish diet, 15 Or breed itself so out of circumstance, That, I being absent, and my place supplied, My general will forget my love and service.
DESDEMONA	Do not doubt that; before Emilia here I give thee warrant of thy place. Assure thee, 20 If I do vow a friendship, I'll perform it To the last article. My lord shall never rest; I'll watch him tame and talk him out of patience; His bed shall seem a school, his board a shrift; I'll intermingle everything he does 25 With Cassio's suit. Therefore be merry, Cassio, For thy solicitor shall rather die Than give thy cause away. *[Enter OTHELLO and IAGO at a distance]*
EMILIA	Madam, here comes my lord.
CASSIO	Madam, I'll take my leave. 30

ACT III, SCENE 3

The castle garden.

[DESDEMONA, CASSIO, and EMILIA enter.]

DESDEMONA   Don't worry, Cassio. I will do my best for you.

EMILIA   Please do, madam. Iago grieves for Cassio's predicament as though it were his own.

DESDEMONA   Oh, Iago is a good man. Don't worry, Cassio. I will rekindle my lord's friendship with you.

CASSIO   Generous lady, whatever happens to me, I will always be your servant.

DESDEMONA   I know and I thank you. You admire Othello. You have known him a long time. Be certain that he will keep his distance from you only so far as to show fairness.

CASSIO   Lady, his distancing may last so long that our relationship weakens. The situation may sap our friendship. When I am gone and someone takes my place, Othello will forget my loyalty and duty to him.

DESDEMONA   Don't think such things. I promise you in front of Emilia, my witness, that you will return to your post. Have faith in my friendship that I will do my best. I will give Othello no rest on the issue. I will keep bringing up your request and will tame his anger. I will turn his bed into a classroom and his dinner table into a religious confessional. I will bring up Cassio's petition in every discussion. Be cheerful, Cassio, for I, your lawyer, would rather die than give up your case. *[OTHELLO and IAGO enter at a distance.]*

EMILIA   Desdemona, here comes Iago.

CASSIO   Lady, I will say goodbye.

ACT III

TRANSLATION

DESDEMONA Why, stay, and hear me speak.

CASSIO Madam, not now: I am very ill at ease,
Unfit for mine own purposes.

DESDEMONA Well, do your discretion. *[Exit CASSIO]*

IAGO Ha! I like not that.

OTHELLO What dost thou say?

IAGO Nothing, my lord; or if—I know not what.

OTHELLO Was not that Cassio parted from my wife?

IAGO Cassio, my lord? No, sure, I cannot think it,
That he would steal away so guilty-like,
Seeing you coming.

OTHELLO I do believe 'twas he.

DESDEMONA How now, my lord?
I have been talking with a suitor here,
A man that languishes in your displeasure.

OTHELLO Who is't you mean?

DESDEMONA Why, your lieutenant, Cassio. Good my lord,
If I have any grace or power to move you,
His present reconciliation take;
For if he be not one that truly loves you,
That errs in ignorance, and not in cunning,
I have no judgment in an honest face.
I prithee call him back.

OTHELLO Went he hence now?

DESDEMONA Yes, faith; so humbled
That he hath left part of his grief with me
To suffer with him. Good love, call him back.

OTHELLO Not now, sweet Desdemona; some other time.

DESDEMONA But shall't be shortly?

OTHELLO The sooner, sweet, for you.

DESDEMONA Shall't be to-night at supper?

OTHELLO No, not to-night.

DESDEMONA To-morrow dinner then?

DESDEMONA	No, stay, and listen to me.
CASSIO	This is not a good time, Lady. I am uncomfortable and unable to plead my case.
DESDEMONA	Do what you think is fitting. *[CASSIO departs.]*
IAGO	Aha! I don't like that.
OTHELLO	What?
IAGO	Nothing, my lord. Perhaps—I don't know what to make of it.
OTHELLO	Wasn't that Cassio departing from Desdemona?
IAGO	Cassio? No, I can't imagine why he would sneak away so guiltily at seeing you approach.
OTHELLO	I believe it was Cassio.
DESDEMONA	How are you, my lord? I have been talking to a man whom you dislike.
OTHELLO	Whom do you mean?
DESDEMONA	Lieutenant Cassio. If I have any influence on your decisions, please reconcile with him. As well as I can judge people, I believe him to be truly friendly, guilty of a mistake, and innocent of deception. Please call him back.
OTHELLO	Did he just leave here?
DESDEMONA	Yes. He departed so demoralized that I feel his grief from listening to his case. Please, dear, reinstate him in the army.
OTHELLO	Not yet, dear Desdemona. Later.
DESDEMONA	But will it be soon?
OTHELLO	I will make it soon just for you, sweetheart.
DESDEMONA	Will you do it tonight at dinner?
OTHELLO	No, not tonight.
DESDEMONA	Tomorrow night at dinner?

ACT III

TRANSLATION

| OTHELLO | I shall not dine at home; |
| | I meet the captains at the citadel. |

DESDEMONA	Why then, to-morrow night, or Tuesday morn,	60
	On Tuesday noon or night, or Wednesday morn.
	I prithee name the time, but let it not
	Exceed three days. I' faith, he's penitent;
	And yet his trespass, in our common reason
	(Save that, they say, the wars must make examples	65
	Out of their best), is not almost a fault
	T' incur a private check. When shall he come?
	Tell me, Othello. I wonder in my soul
	What you could ask me that I should deny
	Or stand so mamm'ring on. What? Michael Cassio,	70
	That came a-wooing with you, and so many a time,
	When I have spoke of you dispraisingly,
	Hath ta'en your part—to have so much to do
	To bring him in? By'r Lady, I could do much—

| OTHELLO | Prithee no more. Let him come when he will! | 75 |
| | I will deny thee nothing. |

DESDEMONA	Why, this is not a boon;
	'Tis as I should entreat you wear your gloves,
	Or feed on nourishing dishes, or keep you warm,
	Or sue to you to do a peculiar profit
	To your own person. Nay, when I have a suit	80
	Wherein I mean to touch your love indeed,
	It shall be full of poise and difficult weight,
	And fearful to be granted.

OTHELLO	I will deny thee nothing!
	Whereon I do beseech thee grant me this,
	To leave me but a little to myself.	85

| DESDEMONA | Shall I deny you? No. Farewell, my lord. |

| OTHELLO | Farewell, my Desdemona: I'll come to thee straight. |

| DESDEMONA | Emilia, come.—Be as your fancies teach you; |
| | Whate'er you be, I am obedient. *[Exit with EMILIA]* |

OTHELLO	Excellent wretch! Perdition catch my soul	90
	But I do love thee! and when I love thee not,
	Chaos is come again.

OTHELLO	I will not be home tomorrow night for dinner. I will meet officers at the fort.
DESDEMONA	Perhaps tomorrow night, or Tuesday morning, or Tuesday midday or night, or Wednesday morning. Choose a time no longer than three days away. He's truly sorry. If it weren't for a time of war, his mistake would be a private matter between commander and second-in-command. When will you talk with him? Tell me, Othello. I wonder what you might ask of me that would make me hesitate. What? Cassio, who accompanied you to my house, often defended you when I criticized you. Why must I struggle to gain him an audience? By the Virgin Mary, I would do anything.

OTHELLO	Please say no more. Let him come whenever he wants! I can never say no to you.
DESDEMONA	This is not a great favor. It is as if I begged you to wear gloves, eat nourishing meals, or stay warm. It is as if I begged you to take care of yourself. When I want a great favor touching your love for me, it will be weightier and more complex and dangerous to grant.
OTHELLO	I can never refuse you anything! I ask only this, leave me in private.
DESDEMONA	Could I refuse? No. Goodbye, my lord.
OTHELLO	Goodbye, my Desdemona. I'll come straight back to you.
DESDEMONA	Come with me, Emilia. Do as you must, Othello. Whatever you demand, I will obey. *[DESDEMONA departs with EMILIA.]*
OTHELLO	Wonderful nag! Hell take my soul if I don't love you! When I stop loving you, the world will fall to ruin.

IAGO	My noble lord—
OTHELLO	What dost thou say, Iago?

IAGO — Did Michael Cassio, when you wooed my lady,
Know of your love?   95

OTHELLO — He did, from first to last. Why dost thou ask?

IAGO — But for a satisfaction of my thought;
No further harm.

OTHELLO — Why of thy thought, Iago?

IAGO — I did not think he had been acquainted with her.

OTHELLO — O, yes, and went between us very oft.   100

IAGO — Indeed?

OTHELLO — Indeed? Ay, indeed! Discern'st thou aught in that?
Is he not honest?

IAGO — Honest, my lord?

OTHELLO — Honest. Ay, honest.

IAGO — My lord, for aught I know.

OTHELLO — What dost thou think?   105

IAGO — Think, my lord?

OTHELLO — Think, my lord?
By heaven, he echoes me,
As if there were some monster in his thought
Too hideous to be shown. Thou dost mean something:
I heard thee say but now, thou lik'st not that,
When Cassio left my wife. What didst not like?   110
And when I told thee he was of my counsel
In my whole course of wooing, thou cried'st 'Indeed?'
And didst contract and purse thy brow together,
As if thou then hadst shut up in thy brain
Some horrible conceit. If thou dost love me,   115
Show me thy thought.

IAGO — My lord, you know I love you.

IAGO	Sir—
OTHELLO	What is it, Iago?
IAGO	When you courted Desdemona, did Cassio know that you loved her?
OTHELLO	He knew all my feelings. Why do you ask?
IAGO	I was just curious. I don't want to cause trouble.
OTHELLO	What are you thinking, Iago?
IAGO	I didn't think Cassio knew Desdemona.
OTHELLO	Oh, yes. He often carried messages from me to her.
IAGO	Really?
OTHELLO	Yes, really! Does that sound strange to you? Isn't Cassio trustworthy?
IAGO	Trustworthy, my lord?
OTHELLO	Trustworthy. Yes, trustworthy.
IAGO	Sir, for all I know he is.
OTHELLO	What are you thinking?
IAGO	Thinking, sir?
OTHELLO	"Thinking, sir?" By God, you repeat me as if you know something too terrible to tell me. You are implying something wrong. I heard you earlier say you didn't approve when Cassio departed from Desdemona. What don't you like? When I told you that I confided in Cassio while I courted Desdemona, you replied, "Really?" You wrinkled your forehead as if to conceal some terrible picture in your mind. If you are my friend, tell me what you suspect.
IAGO	Sir, you know I am your friend.

ACT III

OTHELLO   I think thou dost;
And, for I know thou'rt full of love and honesty
And weigh'st thy words before thou giv'st them breath,
Therefore these stops of thine fright me the more;   120
For such things in a false disloyal knave
Are tricks of custom; but in a man that's just
They are close dilations, working from the heart
That passion cannot rule.

IAGO   For Michael Cassio,
I dare be sworn I think that he is honest.   125

OTHELLO   I think so too.

IAGO   Men should be what they seem;
Or those that be not, would they might seem none!

OTHELLO   Certain, men should be what they seem.

IAGO   Why then, I think Cassio's an honest man.

OTHELLO   Nay, yet there's more in this.   130
I prithee speak to me as to thy thinkings,
As thou dost ruminate, and give thy worst of thoughts
The worst of words.

IAGO   Good my lord, pardon me:
Though I am bound to every act of duty,
I am not bound to that all slaves are free to.   135
Utter my thoughts? Why, say they are vile and false,
As where's that palace whereinto foul things
Sometimes intrude not? Who has a breast so pure
But some uncleanly apprehensions
Keep leets and law days, and in session sit   140
With meditations lawful?

OTHELLO   Thou dost conspire against thy friend, Iago,
If thou but think'st him wronged, and mak'st his ear
A stranger to thy thoughts.

OTHELLO	I believe you are. I believe you friendly and sincere and cautious in thinking before speaking. Your hesitations scare me. Such pauses are common in deceptive rascals. Coming from a worthy man, pauses are secretive and emerge from a heart that emotion can't control.
IAGO	As to Cassio, I swear that I think he is dependable.
OTHELLO	I agree.
IAGO	People should not pretend to be other than their true selves. Those people who deceive are not human at all!
OTHELLO	I agree that people should be straightforward.
IAGO	Well, then, I assume Cassio is honest.
OTHELLO	No. You imply something else. Please tell me what you suspect. As you ponder the question, tell me the worst that you suspect about him.
IAGO	Excuse me, sir. Though I am obedient to military duty, I am not enslaved to the army. Must I tell my private thoughts? What must I do if my thoughts are unclean and faulty? Is there any palace where evil does not slip in? Who is so clean of heart to avoid ugly worries? Who doesn't ponder troubling thoughts?
OTHELLO	You betray your friend, Iago, if you wrong him by concealing your doubts.

ACT III

IAGO   I do beseech you—
Though I perchance am vicious in my guess   145
(As I confess it is my nature's plague
To spy into abuses, and oft my jealousy
Shapes faults that are not), that your wisdom yet
From one that so imperfectly conjects
Would take no notice, nor build yourself a trouble   150
Out of his scattering and unsure observance.
It were not for your quiet nor your good,
Nor for my manhood, honesty, or wisdom,
To let you know my thoughts.

OTHELLO   What dost thou mean?

IAGO   Good name in man and woman, dear my lord,   155
Is the immediate jewel of their souls.
Who steals my purse steals trash; 'tis something, nothing;
'Twas mine, 'tis his, and has been slave to thousands;
But he that filches from me my good name
Robs me of that which not enriches him   160
And makes me poor indeed.

OTHELLO By heaven, I'll know thy thoughts!

IAGO   You cannot, if my heart were in your hand;
Nor shall not whilst 'tis in my custody.

OTHELLO Ha!

IAGO   O, beware, my lord, of jealousy!   165
It is the green-eyed monster, which doth mock
The meat it feeds on. That cuckold lives in bliss
Who, certain of his fate, loves not his wronger;
But O, what damned minutes tells he o'er
Who dotes, yet doubts—suspects, yet strongly loves!   170

OTHELLO O misery!

IAGO   Poor and content is rich, and rich enough;
But riches fineless is as poor as winter
To him that ever fears he shall be poor.
Good God the souls of all my tribe defend   175
From jealousy!

IAGO	I beg you, though I may be wrong in suspecting Cassio. I confess that I tend to look for abuse and often let jealousy imagine faults. You are too wise to be influenced by my faulty logic. Don't trouble yourself with my loose, imperfect observations. It isn't beneficial to your contentment nor does it reflect on my maturity, sincerity, or wisdom for me to speak my concerns.
OTHELLO	What do you mean?
IAGO	The reputation of a man or woman, sir, is the jewel of the soul. Stealing my money is unimportant. Possessions are valueless. They pass from me to the thief and have belonged to thousands of people before. But, the person who slanders me robs me of something that he can't use, but which leaves me poor.
OTHELLO	By God, tell me your thoughts.
IAGO	You couldn't know my thoughts if you held my heart in your hand. You won't know my private thoughts as long as I own my heart.
OTHELLO	Ha!
IAGO	Beware, sir, of suspicion! It is a green-eyed monster that ridicules its victim. The betrayed husband is better off if he is not a friend of his wife's seducer. What wretched minutes he lives when he admires, but doubts a person— when he suspects, but likes his friend!
OTHELLO	Oh suffering!
IAGO	Being poor and comfortable is a form of wealth, a sufficient wealth. But too much wealth is as unpromising as winter to the person who worries about losing his money. God protect my relatives from suspicion!

ACT III

TRANSLATION

OTHELLO	Why, why is this?
	Think'st thou I'ld make a life of jealousy,
	To follow still the changes of the moon
	With fresh suspicions? No! To be once in doubt
	Is once to be resolved. Exchange me for a goat

Why, why is this?
Think'st thou I'ld make a life of jealousy,
To follow still the changes of the moon
With fresh suspicions? No! To be once in doubt
Is once to be resolved. Exchange me for a goat   180
When I shall turn the business of my soul
To such exsufflicate and blown surmises,
Matching thy inference. 'Tis not to make me jealous
To say my wife is fair, feeds well, loves company,
Is free of speech, sings, plays, and dances well;   185
Where virtue is, these are more virtuous.
Nor from mine own weak merits will I draw
The smallest fear or doubt of her revolt,
For she had eyes, and chose me. No, Iago;
I'll see before I doubt; when I doubt, prove;   190
And on the proof there is no more but this—
Away at once with love or jealousy!

IAGO
I am glad of this; for now I shall have reason
To show the love and duty that I bear you
With franker spirit. Therefore, as I am bound,   195
Receive it from me. I speak not yet of proof.
Look to your wife; observe her well with Cassio;
Wear your eye thus, not jealous nor secure:
I would not have your free and noble nature,
Out of self-bounty, be abused. Look to't.   200
I know our country disposition well:
In Venice they do let God see the pranks
They dare not show their husbands; their best conscience
Is not to leave't undone, but keep't unknown.

OTHELLO
Dost thou say so?   205

IAGO
She did deceive her father, marrying you;
And when she seemed to shake and fear your looks,
She loved them most.

OTHELLO   And so she did.

IAGO   Why, go to then!
She that, so young, could give out such a seeming
To seel her father's eyes up close as oak—   210
He thought 'twas witchcraft—but I am much to blame.
I humbly do beseech you of your pardon
For too much loving you.

| OTHELLO | Why are you telling me this? Do you think I would be consumed by suspicion, finding new reasons for doubt each month? No! Once a person falls under suspicion, the situation unleashes a whole lifetime of doubt. You can trade me for a goat when I dedicate myself to odious, contemptible guesses that echo your hints. You don't create jealousy by describing Desdemona as pretty, well fed, vivacious, talkative, and skilled at singing, playing, and dancing. These traits are even better in a good person. I would suspect her of betraying me for my poor qualities. She saw other men, but she chose me. No, Iago. I must see real proof before I doubt Cassio. I will doubt his loyalty only with proof. As to proof, there is none. Stop your hints about love and suspicion! |

| IAGO | I am pleased at your analysis. I have reason to express my friendship and respect with evidence. As a dutiful officer, hear what I have to say. I don't have proof yet. Observe Desdemona, especially when she is with Cassio. Depend on what you see, not on suspicion or trust. Out of generosity to you, I wouldn't want your open-hearted nature ruined. Be alert. I know the Venetian temperament. In Venice, women flirt openly, but conceal their naughtiness from their mates. Their conscience allows them to be disloyal, but forces them to hide their indiscretions. |

ACT III

| OTHELLO | Is that what you think? |

| IAGO | Desdemona tricked Brabantio by eloping with you. When she pretended to tremble at your appearance, she loved you most. |

| OTHELLO | You're right. |

| IAGO | Then consider this! Although young, she fooled her father into believing that you courted her with magic. I take much of the blame. I beg forgiveness for being your friend. |

TRANSLATION

OTHELLO	I am bound to thee for ever.
IAGO	I see this hath a little dashed your spirits.
OTHELLO	Not a jot, not a jot. 215

IAGO
        I' faith, I fear it has.
I hope you will consider what is spoke
Comes from my love. But I do see y' are moved
I am to pray you not to strain my speech
To grosser issues nor to larger reach
Than to suspicion. 220

OTHELLO I will not.

IAGO
        Should you do so, my lord,
My speech should fall into such vile success
As my thoughts aim not at. Cassio's my worthy friend—
My lord, I see y' are moved.

OTHELLO
        No, not much moved:
I do not think but Desdemona's honest. 225

IAGO Long live she so! and long live you to think so!

OTHELLO And yet, how nature erring from itself—

IAGO
Ay, there's the point! as (to be bold with you)
Not to affect many proposed matches
Of her own clime, complexion, and degree, 230
Whereto we see in all things nature tends—
Foh! one may smell in such a will most rank,
Foul disproportion, thoughts unnatural—
But pardon me—I do not in position
Distinctly speak of her; though I may fear 235
Her will, recoiling to her better judgment,
May fall to match you with her country forms,
And happily repent.

OTHELLO
        Farewell, farewell!
If more thou dost perceive, let me know more.
Set on thy wife to observe. Leave me, Iago. 240

IAGO My lord, I take my leave. *[Going]*

OTHELLO
Why did I marry? This honest creature doubtless
Sees and knows more, much more, than he unfolds.

OTHELLO	You are my friend forever.
IAGO	I have crushed your spirit.
OTHELLO	Not a bit.
IAGO	Truly, I think I have. Please take my warning as the word of a friend. I have upset you. Don't read too much into my words to advance from suspecting Desdemona to envisioning worse sins.
OTHELLO	I won't.
IAGO	If you jump to conclusions, sir, my words would push you farther than I intend. Cassio is my good friend. Sir, I make you emotional.
OTHELLO	No, only slightly disturbed. I trust Desdemona's loyalty.
IAGO	May she always be loyal! and may you always trust her!
OTHELLO	And yet, character straying from its nature—
IAGO	Yes, that's the point! I must be bold. People tend to marry mates of their own country, race, and social station. Those who don't, display a waywardness that is bad, out of proportion, and suspect. Excuse me. I can't speak directly of her character. I fear that her desire, straying from her better judgment, may cause her to compare you with white men and, perhaps, to regret marrying you.
OTHELLO	Goodbye! If you observe anything else, tell me. Ask Emilia to spy on Desdemona. Leave me alone, Iago.
IAGO	Sir, I will go. *[IAGO begins departing.]*
OTHELLO	Why did I marry Desdemona? Honest Iago obviously knows more than he is telling me.

ACT III

TRANSLATION

IAGO	*[Returns]* My lord, I would I might entreat your honor
	To scan this thing no further: leave it to time. 245
	Although 'tis fit that Cassio have his place,
	For sure he fills it up with great ability,
	Yet, if you please to hold him off awhile,
	You shall by that perceive him and his means.
	Note if your lady strain his entertainment 250
	With any strong or vehement importunity;
	Much will be seen in that. In the mean time
	Let me be thought too busy in my fears
	(As worthy cause I have to fear I am)
	And hold her free, I do beseech your honor. 255

OTHELLO   Fear not my government.

IAGO   I once more take my leave. *[Exit]*

OTHELLO   This fellow's of exceeding honesty,
And knows all qualities, with a learned spirit
Of human dealings. If I do prove her haggard, 260
Though that her jesses were my dear heartstrings,
I'd whistle her off and let her down the wind
To prey at fortune. Haply, for I am black
And have not those soft parts of conversation
That chamberers have, or for I am declined 265
Into the vale of years—yet that's not much—
She's gone. I am abused, and my relief
Must be to loathe her. O curse of marriage,
That we can call these delicate creatures ours,
And not their appetites! I had rather be a toad 270
And live upon the vapor of a dungeon
Than keep a corner in the thing I love
For others' uses. Yet 'tis the plague of great ones;
Prerogatived are they less than the base.
'Tis destiny unshunnable, like death. 275
Even then this forked plague is fated to us
When we do quicken. Look where she comes.
[Enter DESDEMONA and EMILIA]
If she be false, O, then heaven mocks itself!
I'll not believe't.

DESDEMONA   How now, my dear Othello?
Your dinner, and the generous islanders 280
By you invited, do attend your presence.

IAGO	*[IAGO returns.]* Sir, I beg you to ponder this issue no more. Give it time. Although Cassio deserves to be reinstated because of his ability, delay forgiving him so you can watch him. Notice if Desdemona pleads his case more vehemently. Her enthusiasm will reveal her feelings. Until you know more, please, consider me too suspicious (I have to trust my doubts) and consider Desdemona free of guilt.
OTHELLO	Don't worry about my self-control.
IAGO	Goodbye once more. *[IAGO goes out.]*
OTHELLO	Iago is quite honest and understands human character from his experience with people. If I find Desdemona unfaithful, even though she is tied to my heart, I would abandon her. Maybe because I am black and lack the coy talk of seducers. When I look at advancing age—which is short—I fear I have lost her. I am deceived. My only recourse is to hate her. Oh fault of marriage, that a husband can have a wife, but not control her desires! I would rather be a toad in a drafty dungeon than to share my wife with adulterers. It is the suffering of the privileged. The elite are more likely to suffer infidelity than peasants. I can no more escape my fate than I can avoid death. As soon as we have life, we suffer the plague of disloyalty. Here comes Desdemona now. *[DESDEMONA and EMILIA enter.]* If Desdemona is an adulterer, then God mocks himself by creating a woman who seems so pure. I won't believe the charges against her.
DESDEMONA	How are you, dear Othello? The illustrious islanders you invited to dinner are waiting for you.

ACT III

TRANSLATION

OTHELLO	I am to blame.
DESDEMONA	Why do you speak so faintly? Are you not well?
OTHELLO	I have a pain upon my forehead, here.
DESDEMONA	Faith, that's with watching; 'twill away again. 285 Let me but bind it hard, within this hour It will be well.
OTHELLO	Your napkin is too little; *[He pushes the handkerchief from him, and it falls unnoticed.]* Let it alone. Come, I'll go in with you.
DESDEMONA	I am very sorry that you are not well. *[Exit with OTHELLO]*
EMILIA	I am glad I have found this napkin; 290 This was her first remembrance from the Moor. My wayward husband hath a hundred times Wooed me to steal it; but she so loves the token (For he conjured her she should ever keep it) That she reserves it evermore about her 295 To kiss and talk to. I'll have the work ta'en out And give't Iago. What he will do with it heaven knows, not I; I nothing but to please his fantasy. *[Enter IAGO]*
IAGO	How now? What do you here alone? 300
EMILIA	Do not you chide; I have a thing for you.
IAGO	A thing for me? It is a common thing—
EMILIA	Ha?
IAGO	To have a foolish wife.
EMILIA	O, is that all? What will you give me now 305 For that same handkerchief?
IAGO	What handkerchief?
EMILIA	What handkerchief! Why, that the Moor first gave to Desdemona; That which so often you did bid me steal.
IAGO	Hast stol'n it from her? 310

ORIGINAL

OTHELLO	It's my fault.
DESDEMONA	Why is your voice weak? Are you sick?
OTHELLO	My head hurts.
DESDEMONA	That's from standing watch. It will pass. Let me bind your head and it will stopping hurting in an hour.
OTHELLO	Your cloth is too small. *[He shoves her handkerchief aside. It falls unnoticed by him or her.]* Leave it. I'll go to dinner with you.
DESDEMONA	I am sorry that you are sick. *[She goes out with OTHELLO.]*
EMILIA	I am glad to find this handkerchief. It was one of the first presents that Othello gave her. My mischievous husband has asked me to steal it a hundred times. But Desdemona loves it. Othello instructed her to keep it forever. Desdemona keeps the handkerchief with her always to kiss and whisper to. I will have an embroiderer copy it and give the copy to Iago. I don't know what he will do with it. I obey him only to please his whim. *[IAGO enters.]*

ACT III

IAGO	What are you doing? Why are you in the garden alone?
EMILIA	Don't fuss. I have something for you.
IAGO	Something for me? It is not unusual—
EMILIA	Yes?
IAGO	To have a silly wife.
EMILIA	Is that all you have to say? What will you give me for a copy of the handkerchief?
IAGO	What handkerchief?
EMILIA	What handkerchief! The first gift that Othello gave Desdemona. The one you have often ordered me to steal for you.
IAGO	Did you steal it from her?

EMILIA	No, faith; she let it drop by negligence,
	And to th' advantage, I, being here, took't up.
	Look, here it is.
IAGO	A good wench! Give it me.
EMILIA	What will you do with't, that you have been so earnest
	To have me filch it? 315
IAGO	Why, what's that to you?
	[Snatches it]
EMILIA	If it be not for some purpose of import,
	Give't me again. Poor lady, she'll run mad
	When she shall lack it.
IAGO	Be not acknown on't; I have use for it.
	Go, leave me. *[Exit EMILIA]* 320
	I will in Cassio's lodging lose this napkin
	And let him find it. Trifles light as air
	Are to the jealous confirmations strong
	As proofs of holy writ. This may do something.
	The Moor already changes with my poison: 325
	Dangerous conceits are in their natures poisons,
	Which at the first are scarce found to distaste,
	But with a little act upon the blood
	Burn like the mines of sulphur.
	[Enter OTHELLO]
	I did say so.
	Look where he comes! Not poppy nor mandragora, 330
	Nor all the drowsy syrups of the world,
	Shall ever med'cine thee to that sweet sleep
	Which thou owedst yesterday.
OTHELLO	Ha! ha! false to me?
IAGO	Why, how now, general? No more of that!
OTHELLO	Avaunt! be gone! Thou hast set me on the rack. 335
	I swear 'tis better to be much abused
	Than but to know't a little.
IAGO	How now, my lord?

EMILIA	No. Truly, she dropped it by accident. Luckily, I picked it up. See, here it is.
IAGO	Good girl! Hand it here.
EMILIA	What will you do with a handkerchief that you wanted stolen?
IAGO	Why is that your business? *[IAGO snatches the handkerchief.]*
EMILIA	If it isn't important to you, give it back. Poor woman, she'll be distraught when she finds it gone.
IAGO	Pretend you know nothing about it. I need it. Go away. Leave me. *[EMILIA goes out.]* I will put this in Cassio's room for him to find. Small items are as strong evidence to the suspicious as works of scripture. This may be useful. I have already poisoned Othello's thinking about Desdemona. Fantasies are poisonous. At first, the victim barely notices the taste. When the poison reaches the bloodstream, fantasies burn like sulfur mines. *[OTHELLO enters.]* It's just as I said. Here comes Othello! No sleeping potion of the poppy, mandrake, or world drugs can restore the pleasant rest you enjoyed yesterday.
OTHELLO	Ah! Is she unfaithful to me?
IAGO	Please, sir. No more worry about that!
OTHELLO	Go! Depart! You have tortured me on the rack. It is better to be tormented than to be teased with a small suspicion.
IAGO	What has happened, sir?

ACT III

OTHELLO	What sense had I of her stol'n hours of lust?
	I saw't not, thought it not, it harmed not me;
	I slept the next night well, fed well, was free and merry; 340
	I found not Cassio's kisses on her lips.
	He that is robbed, not wanting what is stol'n,
	Let him not know't, and he's not robbed at all.

| IAGO | I am sorry to hear this. |

OTHELLO	I had been happy if the general camp, 345
	Pioners and all, had tasted her sweet body,
	So I had nothing known. O, now for ever
	Farewell the tranquil mind! farewell content!
	Farewell the plumed troop, and the big wars
	That make ambition virtue! O, farewell! 350
	Farewell the neighing steed and the shrill trump,
	The spirit-stirring drum, th' ear-piercing fife,
	The royal banner, and all quality,
	Pride, pomp, and circumstance of glorious war!
	And O you mortal engines whose rude throats 355
	Th' immortal Jove's dread clamors counterfeit,
	Farewell! Othello's occupation's gone!

| IAGO | Is't possible, my lord? |

OTHELLO	Villain, be sure thou prove my love a whore!
	Be sure of it; give me the ocular proof; 360
	Or, by the worth of man's eternal soul,
	Thou hadst been better have been born a dog
	Than answer my waked wrath!

| IAGO | Is't come to this? |

OTHELLO	Make me to see't; or at the least so prove it
	That the probation bear no hinge nor loop 365
	To hang a doubt on—or woe upon thy life!

| IAGO | My noble lord— |

OTHELLO	If thou dost slander her and torture me,
	Never pray more; abandon all remorse;
	On horror's head horrors accumulate; 370
	Do deeds to make heaven weep, all earth amazed;
	For nothing canst thou to damnation add
	Greater than that.

OTHELLO	What did I know about her stolen hours with a lover? I didn't see it, didn't think it, wasn't hurt by it. The next night, I slept peacefully, ate well, felt happy and untroubled. I didn't envision Cassio kissing Desdemona. It is better not to know about theft. Then the victim does not feel cheated.
IAGO	I am sorry to hear your words.
OTHELLO	I would have been content if every man in the camp, even the ditch diggers, had enjoyed her body if I had not known about it. Now, goodbye to peaceful thoughts forever. Goodbye peace! Goodbye to a career based on uniformed regiments and great wars. Oh, goodbye! Goodbye the war horse, the trumpet alarms, the dramatic drum, the high-pitched fife, the royal flag, and all traits, pride, order, and scenes of war's glories. And all the artillery that sounds like Jupiter's thunder, goodbye. Othello has given up his career!
IAGO	Is it possible, sir?
OTHELLO	Rogue, you must prove your charge that my Desdemona is a whore! Be certain. Give me visible proof. By the value of the soul, you would be better off born a dog than to face my rage!
IAGO	Have you come to this?
OTHELLO	Show it to me. If you can't prove your charge, I will kill you!
IAGO	Noble sir—
OTHELLO	If you lie about her to harm me, give up praying. Give up regret. I will heap horror on horror to punish you. I will commit crimes that make the skies weep and the earth marvel. You can't add any more to your doom than that.

ACT III

IAGO	O grace! O heaven forgive me!
	Are you a man? Have you a soul or sense?—
	God b' wi' you! take mine office. O wretched fool, 375
	That liv'st to make thine honesty a vice!
	A monstrous world! Take note, take note, O world,
	To be direct and honest is not safe.
	I thank you for this profit; and from hence
	I'll love no friend, sith love breeds such offense. 380
OTHELLO	Nay, stay. Thou shouldst be honest.
IAGO	I should be wise; for honesty's a fool
	And loses that it works for.
OTHELLO	By the world,
	I think my wife be honest, and think she is not;
	I think that thou art just, and think thou art not. 385
	I'll have some proof. Her name, that was as fresh
	As Dian's visage, is now begrimed and black
	As mine own face. If there be cords, or knives,
	Poison, or fire, or suffocating streams,
	I'll not endure it. Would I were satisfied! 390
IAGO	I see, sir, you are eaten up with passion:
	I do repent me that I put it to you.
	You would be satisfied?
OTHELLO	Would? Nay, I will.
IAGO	And may; but how? how satisfied, my lord?
	Would you, the supervisor, grossly gape on? 395
	Behold her topped?
OTHELLO	Death and damnation! O!
IAGO	It were a tedious difficulty, I think,
	To bring them to that prospect. Damn them then,
	If ever mortal eyes do see them bolster
	More than their own! What then? How then? 400
	What shall I say? Where's satisfaction?
	It is impossible you should see this,
	Were they as prime as goats, as hot as monkeys,
	As salt as wolves in pride, and fools as gross
	As ignorance made drunk. But yet, I say, 405
	If imputation and strong circumstances
	Which lead directly to the door of truth
	Will give you satisfaction, you may have't.

ORIGINAL

IAGO	Oh, God's grace! Oh, heaven forgive me! Are you human? Do you possess a soul and intelligence? Goodbye! Take back my military post. Oh, stupid lout, you have turned candor into a crime! Oh, cruel world! Notice, oh, world, that it is not safe to be straightforward and honest. I thank you, Othello, for teaching me this truth. From now on, I want no comrade, because friendship leads to great harm.
OTHELLO	No, don't say that. You should be truthful.
IAGO	I would rather be wise. It is foolish to be candid and to fail to accomplish anything.
OTHELLO	According to worldly wisdom, I both trust and doubt my wife's fidelity. I both trust and doubt you. I demand proof of Desdemona's fault. Her name, that was as pure as the face of Diana, the goddess of chastity, is now blackened as dark as my face. If I can find rope, knives, poison, fire, or water to drown in, I don't want to live. How can I be satisfied!
IAGO	I see, sir, that passion devours you. I regret telling you about Desdemona and Cassio. Do you want vengeance?
OTHELLO	Want? No, I will have it.
IAGO	You may find vengeance, but how? How can revenge content you, sir? Would you, the husband, spy on the lovers? Would you watch her beneath Cassio?
OTHELLO	Death and doom! Oh!
IAGO	It would be complicated to catch Desdemona and Cassio making love. Damn them both if any witness see them in bed together. What will you do then? What is your next move? What can I tell you? What satisfaction will evidence give you? It is inadvisable for you to see them, if they were as randy as goats, as lustful as monkeys, as desirous as wolves with a pack of females, and as foolish as lovers who don't know they are watched. I promise, if personal and physical evidence lead you to truth and satisfy your mind, you shall have it.

ACT III

OTHELLO	Give me a living reason she's disloyal.	
IAGO	I do not like the office.	410
	But sith I am entered in this cause so far,	
	Pricked to't by foolish honesty and love,	
	I will go on. I lay with Cassio lately,	
	And being troubled with a raging tooth,	
	I could not sleep.	415
	There are a kind of men so loose of soul	
	That in their sleeps will mutter their affairs.	
	One of this kind is Cassio.	
	In sleep I heard him say, 'Sweet Desdemona,	
	Let us be wary, let us bide our loves!'	420
	And then, sir, would he gripe and wring my hand,	
	Cry 'O sweet creature!' and then kiss me hard,	
	As if he plucked up kisses by the roots	
	That grew upon my lips; then laid his leg	
	Over my thigh, and sighed, and kissed, and then	425
	Cried 'Cursed fate that gave thee to the Moor!'	
OTHELLO	O monstrous! monstrous!	
IAGO	Nay, this was but his dream.	
OTHELLO	But this denoted a foregone conclusion:	
	'Tis a shrewd doubt, though it be but a dream.	
IAGO	And this may help to thicken other proofs	430
	That do demonstrate thinly.	
OTHELLO	I'll tear her all to pieces!	
IAGO	Nay, but be wise. Yet we see nothing done;	
	She may be honest yet. Tell me but this—	
	Have you not sometimes seen a handkerchief	435
	Spotted with strawberries in your wife's hand?	
OTHELLO	I gave her such a one; 'twas my first gift.	
IAGO	I know not that; but such a handkerchief—	
	I am sure it was your wife's—did I to-day	
	See Cassio wipe his beard with.	440
OTHELLO	If't be that—	
IAGO	If it be that, or any that was hers,	
	It speaks against her with the other proofs.	

OTHELLO   Give me undeniable proof that she's unfaithful.

IAGO   I don't like the assignment. Since I have gone this far in informing you, urged on by sincerity and friendship, I will find proof. I shared a bed with Cassio recently. I couldn't sleep because of a toothache. Some men are so free of concealment that they talk in their sleep about their sexual conquests. Cassio is one of these. While he slept, he said, "Sweet Desdemona, let's be careful, let's put off our affair!" Then, sir, he grabbed my hand, moaned "Oh, sweet creature," and kissed me hard as if he yanked kisses like plants growing out of my lips. He thrust his leg across my thigh and sighed and kissed me. He cried out, "I curse destiny for giving you to Othello!"

OTHELLO   Oh, horrible, horrible!

IAGO   But Cassio was only dreaming.

OTHELLO   He was re-enacting a real event. It is suspicious, even though he was only dreaming.

IAGO   This dream may substantiate my weaker evidence.

OTHELLO   I'll tear her apart!

IAGO   No, get hold of yourself. We have no visible evidence. She may be innocent. Tell me, have you sometime seen Desdemona holding a handkerchief decorated with strawberries?

OTHELLO   I gave her one like that as a first gift.

IAGO   I didn't know about that. I saw Cassio wipe his beard today with a handkerchief that belongs to Desdemona.

OTHELLO   If this is true—

IAGO   If it was the handkerchief you gave her or any other of hers, it adds to proof of her sin.

ACT III

TRANSLATION

OTHELLO	O, that the slave had forty thousand lives!
	One is too poor, too weak for my revenge.
	Now do I see 'tis true. Look here, Iago: 445
	All my fond love thus do I blow to heaven. 'Tis gone.
	Arise, black vengeance, from the hollow hell!
	Yield up, O love, thy crown and hearted throne
	To tyrannous hate! Swell, bosom, with thy fraught,
	For 'tis of aspics' tongues! 450
IAGO	Yet be content.
OTHELLO	O, blood, blood, blood!
IAGO	Patience, I say. Your mind perhaps may change.
OTHELLO	Never, Iago. Like to the Pontic sea,
	Whose icy current and compulsive course
	Ne'er feels retiring ebb, but keeps due on 455
	To the Propontic and the Hellespont,
	Even so my bloody thoughts, with violent pace,
	Shall ne'er look back, ne'er ebb to humble love,
	Till that a capable and wide revenge
	Swallow them up. *[He kneels]* Now, by yond marble heaven, 460
	In the due reverence of a sacred vow
	I here engage my words.
IAGO	Do not rise. *[Iago kneels]*
	Witness, you ever-burning lights above,
	You elements that clip us round about,
	Witness that here Iago doth give up 465
	The execution of his wit, hands, heart
	To wronged Othello's service! Let him command,
	And to obey shall be in me remorse,
	What bloody business ever. *[They rise]*
OTHELLO	I greet thy love,
	Not with vain thanks but with acceptance bounteous, 470
	And will upon the instant put thee to't.
	Within these three days let me hear thee say
	That Cassio's not alive.
IAGO	My friend is dead; 'tis done at your request.
	But let her live. 475

OTHELLO	Oh, I wish Cassio had forty thousand lives! I can only kill him once in vengeance. I am convinced. Iago, I banish to the skies all my fondness for Desdemona. Our marriage is over. Hell's vengeance arises! Love, give up your place to rage! Heart, swell with the venom of snakes' tongues!
IAGO	Be at peace.
OTHELLO	I want blood.
IAGO	Be patient. You may change your mind.
OTHELLO	I won't, Iago. Just as the cold Black Sea never stops its tide but presses on to the Sea of Marmora and the Bosporus Strait, my destructive thoughts never turn back from violence. My rage never gives place to affection until vengeance devours both hate and love. *[OTHELLO kneels.]* By heaven, I pledge to keep my vow.
IAGO	Don't get up. *[IAGO kneels.]* Witness, stars and elements that surround us, Iago pledges his thoughts, hands, and heart to help Othello right this wrong. Let Othello order me to any bloody job. *[OTHELLO and IAGO rise.]*
OTHELLO	I welcome your friendship, not with idle thanks, but with great-hearted acceptance. I will immediately put you to work. Within a span of three days, kill Cassio.
IAGO	I will kill my friend Cassio as you ask. Don't kill Desdemona.

ACT III

TRANSLATION

OTHELLO   Damn her, lewd minx! O, damn her!
Come, go with me apart. I will withdraw
To furnish me with some swift means of death
For the fair devil. Now art thou my lieutenant.

IAGO   I am your own for ever. *[Exeunt]*

OTHELLO   Damn her, trashy flirt! Oh, damn her! Speak with me in private. I will think up some quick way of killing her. You are now promoted to lieutenant.

IAGO   I am your friend forever. *[IAGO and OTHELLO depart.]*

ACT III, SCENE 4

Before the castle.

[Enter DESDEMONA, EMILIA, and Clown]

DESDEMONA   Do you know, sirrah, where Lieutenant
Cassio lies?

CLOWN   I dare not say he lies anywhere.

DESDEMONA   Why, man?

CLOWN   He's a soldier, and for me to say a soldier   5
lies is stabbing.

DESDEMONA   Go to. Where lodges he?

CLOWN   To tell you where he lodges is to tell you
where I lie.

DESDEMONA   Can anything be made of this?   10

CLOWN   I know not where he lodges; and for me to
devise a lodging, and say he lies here or he lies
there, were to lie in mine own throat.

DESDEMONA   Can you enquire him out, and be edified
by report?   15

CLOWN   I will catechize the world for him; that is,
make questions, and by them answer.

DESDEMONA   Seek him, bid him come hither. Tell
him I have moved my lord on his behalf and hope all
will be well.   20

CLOWN   To do this is within the compass of man's
wit, and therefore I'll attempt the doing of it. *[Exit]*

DESDEMONA   Where should I lose that handkerchief,
Emilia?

EMILIA   I know not, madam.   25

ACT III, SCENE 4

In front of the castle in Cyprus.

[DESDEMONA, EMILIA, and the clown enter.]

DESDEMONA   Do you know, sir, where Lieutenant Cassio lies?

CLOWN   I don't charge him with lying anywhere.

DESDEMONA   Why not?

CLOWN   He's a soldier. I would be stabbing him if I say he lies.

DESDEMONA   Nonsense. Where is his room?

CLOWN   To reveal his room is to tell you where I lie.

DESDEMONA   Can I make any sense of this?

CLOWN   I don't know where his room is. To make up a location and say he lies here or there would make me a liar.

DESDEMONA   Will you ask around?

CLOWN   I will search the world by asking and getting answers.

DESDEMONA   Find him and tell him to come here. Tell him I have convinced Othello of Cassio's case and hope to repair their broken friendship.

CLOWN   Any man could accomplish this, so I will try. *[He goes out.]*

DESDEMONA   Where could I have misplaced my handkerchief, Emilia?

EMILIA   I don't know, ma'am.

TRANSLATION

DESDEMONA	Believe me, I had rather have lost my purse Full of crusadoes; and but my noble Moor Is true of mind, and made of no such baseness As jealous creatures are, it were enough To put him to ill thinking. 30
EMILIA	Is he not jealous?
DESDEMONA	Who? he? I think the sun where he was born Drew all such humors from him. *[Enter OTHELLO]*
EMILIA	Look where he comes.
DESDEMONA	I will not leave him now till Cassio Be called to him.—How is't with you, my lord?
OTHELLO	Well, my good lady. *[Aside]* O, hardness to dissemble! 35 How do you, Desdemona?
DESDEMONA	Well, my good lord.
OTHELLO	Give me your hand. This hand is moist, my lady.
DESDEMONA	It yet hath felt no age nor known no sorrow.
OTHELLO	This argues fruitfulness and liberal heart. Hot, hot, and moist. This hand of yours requires 40 A sequester from liberty, fasting and prayer, Much castigation, exercise devout; For here's a young and sweating devil here That commonly rebels. 'Tis a good hand, A frank one. 45
DESDEMONA	You may, indeed, say so; For 'twas that hand that gave away my heart.
OTHELLO	A liberal hand! The hearts of old gave hands; But our new heraldry is hands, not hearts.
DESDEMONA	I cannot speak of this. Come now, your promise!
OTHELLO	What promise, chuck? 50
DESDEMONA	I have sent to bid Cassio come speak with you.
OTHELLO	I have a salt and sorry rheum offends me. Lend me thy handkerchief.
DESDEMONA	Here, my lord.

ORIGINAL

DESDEMONA	I would rather have lost a purse filled with gold coins. If Othello were not so honest and decent a man, the loss might make him doubt me.
EMILIA	Isn't he jealous?
DESDEMONA	Othello? I think the sun baked evil out of him at birth. *[OTHELLO enters.]*
EMILIA	See, here he comes.
DESDEMONA	I will stay with him until Cassio arrives. How are you, my lord?
OTHELLO	Feeling better, my wife. *[To himself]* Oh, it is difficult to pretend! How are you, Desdemona?
DESDEMONA	I am well, sir.
OTHELLO	Give me your hand. It is damp, my lady.
DESDEMONA	It has never suffered old age or grief.
OTHELLO	You describe a person who is productive and generous. Warm and damp. Your hand requires confinement, fasting, and prayer, much scolding, and practice in religious devotion. There is temptation here that may rebel against righteousness. You have a good hand, a straightforward one.
DESDEMONA	You are right. It was that hand that gave you my heart.
OTHELLO	A free hand! People used to pledge with handshakes, but now they give their hands without sincerity.
DESDEMONA	I don't know anything about your claim. Please, you gave me your word!
OTHELLO	What did I promise, my dear?
DESDEMONA	I sent for Cassio to plead his case to you.
OTHELLO	I have a head cold that troubles me. Lend me your handkerchief.
DESDEMONA	Here is one, my lord.

ACT III

TRANSLATION

OTHELLO	That which I gave you.
DESDEMONA	I have it not about me.
OTHELLO	Not?
DESDEMONA	No, faith, my lord.
OTHELLO	That is a fault.

That handkerchief
Did an Egyptian to my mother give.
She was a charmer, and could almost read
The thoughts of people. She told her, while she kept it,
'Twould make her amiable and subdue my father
Entirely to her love; but if she lost it
Or made a gift of it, my father's eye
Should hold her loathly, and his spirits should hunt
After new fancies. She, dying, gave it me,
And bid me, when my fate would have me wive,
To give it her. I did so; and take heed on't;
Make it a darling like your precious eye.
To lose't or give't away were such perdition
As nothing else could match.

DESDEMONA	Is't possible?
OTHELLO	'Tis true. There's magic in the web of it.

A sibyl that had numbered in the world
The sun to course two hundred compasses,
In her prophetic fury sewed the work;
The worms were hallowed that did breed the silk;
And it was dyed in mummy which the skillful
Conserved of maidens' hearts.

DESDEMONA	I' faith? Is't true?
OTHELLO	Most veritable. Therefore look to't well.
DESDEMONA	Then would to God that I had never seen't!
OTHELLO	Ha! Wherefore?
DESDEMONA	Why do you speak so startingly and rash?
OTHELLO	Is't lost? Is't gone? Speak, is it out o' th' way?
DESDEMONA	Heaven bless us!
OTHELLO	Say you?

55

60

65

70

75

80

ORIGINAL

OTHELLO	I want the one I gave you.
DESDEMONA	I don't have it with me.
OTHELLO	No?
DESDEMONA	No, my lord.
OTHELLO	That is too bad. An Egyptian gave that handkerchief to my mother. The Egyptian was a magician who read people's thoughts. The Egyptian told my mother that the handkerchief would make my mother lovable and would control my father with her affection. If my mother lost the handkerchief or gave it away, my father would hate her. He would look for new romances. My mother, on her deathbed, gave the handkerchief to me. She instructed me to give it to my future wife. I did as she instructed. Watch out for the handkerchief. Make it as precious as your eye. To lose or give up the handkerchief would cause you more doom than anything else could.
DESDEMONA	Do you believe the Egyptian's words?
OTHELLO	She told the truth. The handkerchief is woven with magic. A 200-year-old prophet embroidered the handkerchief. Holy silkworms made the thread. The preserved liquid from virgins' hearts dyed the handkerchief.
DESDEMONA	Really? Are you telling the truth?
OTHELLO	Truly. Look after the handkerchief.
DESDEMONA	I wish to God I had never seen it!
OTHELLO	Why?
DESDEMONA	Why do you sound so abrupt and shocked?
OTHELLO	Have you lost it? Is it gone? Tell me, is it mislaid?
DESDEMONA	Heaven help us!
OTHELLO	Is that what you are telling me?

ACT III

DESDEMONA	It is not lost. But what an if it were?
OTHELLO	How?
DESDEMONA	I say it is not lost.
OTHELLO	Fetch't, let me see't!
DESDEMONA	Why, so I can, sir; but I will not now. This is a trick to put me from my suit: Pray you let Cassio be received again.
OTHELLO	Fetch me the handkerchief! My mind misgives.
DESDEMONA	Come, come! You'll never meet a more sufficient man.
OTHELLO	The handkerchief!
DESDEMONA	I pray talk me of Cassio.
OTHELLO	The handkerchief!
DESDEMONA	A man that all his time Hath founded his good fortunes on your love, Shared dangers with you—
OTHELLO	The handkerchief!
DESDEMONA	Faith, you are to blame.
OTHELLO	Zounds! *[Exit]*
EMILIA	Is not this man jealous?
DESDEMONA	I ne'er saw this before. Sure there's some wonder in this handkerchief; I am most unhappy in the loss of it.
EMILIA	'Tis not a year or two shows us a man. They are all but stomachs, and we all but food; They eat us hungerly, and when they are full, They belch us. *[Enter IAGO and CASSIO]* Look you—Cassio and my husband!
IAGO	There is no other way; It is she must do't. And lo the happiness! Go and importune her.

85

90

95

100

105

ORIGINAL

DESDEMONA	It isn't lost. What would you say if it did lose it?
OTHELLO	What?
DESDEMONA	It isn't lost.
OTHELLO	Bring it here. I want to see it!
DESDEMONA	I can locate it, but not now. You are distracting me from my request. Please speak again with Cassio.
OTHELLO	Bring me the handkerchief. I am concerned for it.
DESDEMONA	Please! You will never meet a worthier man.
OTHELLO	Bring the handkerchief!
DESDEMONA	Let's talk about Cassio.
OTHELLO	Bring the handkerchief!
DESDEMONA	Cassio risked his career on your friendship, shared danger with you—
OTHELLO	Bring the handkerchief!
DESDEMONA	Truly, it's your fault.
OTHELLO	God's wounds! *[OTHELLO goes out.]*
EMILIA	Isn't Othello suspicious?
DESDEMONA	I have never seen him like this. There is something unusual about the handkerchief. I was unlucky to lose it.
EMILIA	We can't learn everything about a man in a year or two. Men are hungry and use us like food. They gobble us up. When they are satisfied, they regurgitate us. *[IAGO and CASSIO enter.]* Look—Cassio and Iago!
IAGO	There is no other solution. Desdemona must intercede with Othello. She can bring you happiness! Go and ask her.

ACT III

TRANSLATION

DESDEMONA	How now, good Cassio? What's the news with you? 110
CASSIO	Madam, my former suit. I do beseech you That by your virtuous means I may again Exist, and be a member of his love Whom I with all the office of my heart Entirely honor. I would not be delayed. 115 If my offense be of such mortal kind That neither service past, nor present sorrows, Nor purposed merit in futurity, Can ransom me into his love again, But to know so must be my benefit. 120 So shall I clothe me in a forced content, And shut myself up in some other course, To fortune's alms.
DESDEMONA	Alas, thrice-gentle Cassio! My advocation is not now in tune. My lord is not my lord; nor should I know him, 125 Were he in favor as in humor altered. So help me every spirit sanctified As I have spoken for you all my best And stood within the blank of his displeasure For my free speech! You must awhile be patient. 130 What I can do I will; and more I will Than for myself I dare. Let that suffice you.
IAGO	Is my lord angry?
EMILIA	He went hence but now, And certainly in strange unquietness.
IAGO	Can he be angry? I have seen the cannon 135 When it hath blown his ranks into the air And, like the devil, from his very arm Puffed his own brother—and can he be angry? Something of moment then. I will go meet him. There's matter in't indeed if he be angry. 140

DESDEMONA	How are you, Cassio? What is happening with you?
CASSIO	Lady, my previous request. Please use your kindness to make me live again and to be a comrade to him whom I honor with all my heart. I don't want to delay my case. If my fault is so self-destructive that my past record, present pain, and future worth to the army cannot retrieve his friendship, I want to know. I will force myself to be satisfied and choose a new way to earn my destiny.
DESDEMONA	I'm sorry, gentle Cassio! I have lost my power over Othello. He is not himself. He is so out of humor that I don't recognize him. May angels help me, I have pleaded on your behalf and gained his anger for speaking so openly! Be patient. I will do what I can. I will work harder for you than for myself. Let that be enough.
IAGO	Is Othello mad at you?
EMILIA	He just left in a strange mood.
IAGO	Is he angry? I have seen him in the midst of cannon fire, which ripped his brother from his side—can Othello be angry? It is only temporary. I will talk with him. There must be something serious to make him mad.

ACT III

DESDEMONA	I prithee do so. *[Exit IAGO]*
	Something sure of state,
	Either from Venice or some unhatched practice
	Made demonstrable here in Cyprus to him,
	Hath puddled his clear spirit; and in such cases
	Men's natures wrangle with inferior things, 145
	Though great ones are their object. 'Tis even so;
	For let our finger ache, and it endues
	Our other, healthful members even to that sense
	Of pain. Nay, we must think men are not gods,
	Nor of them look for such observancy 150
	As fits the bridal. Beshrew me much, Emilia,
	I was, unhandsome warrior as I am,
	Arraigning his unkindness with my soul;
	But now I find I had suborned the witness,
	And he's indicted falsely. 155
EMILIA	Pray heaven it be state matters, as you think,
	And no conception nor no jealous toy
	Concerning you.
DESDEMONA	Alas the day! I never gave him cause.
EMILIA	But jealous souls will not be answered so; 160
	They are not ever jealous for the cause,
	But jealous for they are jealous. 'Tis a monster
	Begot upon itself, born on itself.
DESDEMONA	Heaven keep that monster from Othello's mind!
EMILIA	Lady, amen. 165
DESDEMONA	I will go seek him. Cassio, walk here about:
	If I do find him, I'll move your suit
	And seek to effect it to my uttermost.
CASSIO	I humbly thank your ladyship.
	[Exeunt DESDEMONA and EMILIA]
	[Enter BIANCA]
BIANCA	Save you, friend Cassio! 170
CASSIO	What make you from home?
	How is it with you, my most fair Bianca?
	I' faith, sweet love, I was coming to your house.

ORIGINAL

DESDEMONA	Please talk to him. *[IAGO goes out.]* Some government matter from Venice or from an uncompleted battle plan set to be executed in Cyprus has muddled his thinking. In these situations, men worry over surface matters rather than over the real issues. It is always this way. If one finger throbs, it causes the other fingers to share the pain. We must realize that men are not divine. We shouldn't expect them to act like considerate grooms to their brides. Curse me, Emilia, I was unfairly charging him with judging me. I have forced him into a lie and falsely accused him for it.
EMILIA	I pray that state matters worry him. I hope that he has no false view or suspicious fantasy about you.
DESDEMONA	Oh, no! I give him no reason to be angry.
EMILIA	Reason does not control jealousy. Jealousy is not based on real causes. Jealousy arises from itself. It is a monster born of its own siring.
DESDEMONA	God keep jealousy out of Othello's mind!
EMILIA	So be it, Lady.
DESDEMONA	I will look for him. Cassio, stay here. If I find Othello, I will press your request as far as I can.
CASSIO	I humbly thank you, Lady. *[DESDEMONA and EMILIA go out.]* *[BIANCA enters.]*
BIANCA	God save you, Cassio!
CASSIO	Why did you leave home? How are you, beautiful Bianca? Sweetheart, I was on my way to your house.

ACT III

TRANSLATION

BIANCA	And I was going to your lodging, Cassio.
	What, keep a week away? seven days and nights?
	Eightscore eight hours? and lovers' absent hours, 175
	More tedious than the dial eightscore times?
	O weary reck'ning!
CASSIO	Pardon me, Bianca:
	I have this while with leaden thoughts been pressed;
	But I shall in a more continuate time
	Strike off this score of absence. Sweet Bianca. 180
	[Gives her DESDEMONA's handkerchief]
	Take me this work out.
BIANCA	O Cassio, whence came this?
	This is some token from a newer friend.
	To the felt absence now I feel a cause.
	Is't come to this? Well, well.
CASSIO	Go to, woman!
	Throw your vile guesses in the devil's teeth, 185
	From whence you have them. You are jealous now
	That this is from some mistress, some remembrance.
	No, by my faith, Bianca.
BIANCA	Why, whose is it?
CASSIO	I know not, sweet; I found it in my chamber.
	I like the work well; ere it be demanded, 190
	As like enough it will, I'd have it copied.
	Take it and do't, and leave me for this time.
BIANCA	Leave you? Wherefore?
CASSIO	I do attend here on the general
	And think it no addition, nor my wish, 195
	To have him see me womaned.
BIANCA	Why, I pray you?
CASSIO	Not that I love you not.
BIANCA	But that you do not love me!
	I pray you bring me on the way a little,
	And say if I shall see you soon at night.
CASSIO	'Tis but a little way that I can bring you, 200
	For I attend here; but I'll see you soon.
BIANCA	'Tis very good. I must be circumstanced.
	[Exeunt]

BIANCA	And I was coming to your room, Cassio. Why have you been gone for a week—seven days and nights, 168 hours? For lovers, the time apart is even longer. I am tired of counting the time.
CASSIO	Excuse me, Bianca. I have had worries to deal with. I shall spend uninterrupted time with you to make up for my absence, sweet Bianca. *[CASSIO gives BIANCA DESDEMONA's handkerchief.]* Copy this embroidery.
BIANCA	Cassio, where did you get this handkerchief? It is a love token from a new girlfriend. Now I know why you have been gone. Have you begun sneaking around? Well.
CASSIO	Nonsense, woman! Toss your suspicions back to the devil they came from. You suspect that this handkerchief is a token from a mistress. Truly, it isn't, Bianca.
BIANCA	Then, whose is it?
CASSIO	I don't know, sweetheart. I found it in my room. I admire the pattern. Before I find the owner, please copy the embroidery. Take it with you and leave me for a time.
BIANCA	Why should I leave you?
CASSIO	I am waiting to see General Othello. I don't want him to find me with a woman.
BIANCA	Why not?
CASSIO	Not because I don't love you.
BIANCA	You don't love me! Accompany me a short distance and tell me you will see me tonight.
CASSIO	I can walk only a short way. I must wait here, but I will see you soon.
BIANCA	Good. I understand the situation. *[CASSIO and BIANCA depart.]*

ACT III

TRANSLATION

ACT IV, SCENE 1

The same.

[Enter OTHELLO and IAGO]

IAGO   Will you think so?

OTHELLO   Think so, Iago?

IAGO   What,
          To kiss in private?

OTHELLO   An unauthorized kiss.

IAGO   Or to be naked with her friend in bed
          An hour or more, not meaning any harm?

OTHELLO   Naked in bed, Iago, and not mean harm?   5
          It is hypocrisy against the devil
          They that mean virtuously, and yet do so,
          The devil their virtue tempts, and they tempt heaven.

IAGO   So they do nothing, 'tis a venial slip.
          But if I give my wife a handkerchief—   10

OTHELLO   What then?

IAGO   Why, then 'tis hers, my lord; and being hers,
          She may, I think, bestow't on any man.

OTHELLO   She is protectress of her honor too;
          May she give that?   15

IAGO   Her honor is an essence that's not seen;
          They have it very oft that have it not.
          But for the handkerchief—

OTHELLO   By heaven, I would most gladly have forgot it!
          Thou said'st—O, it comes o'er my memory   20
          As doth the raven o'er the infected house,
          Boding to all!—he had my handkerchief.

IAGO   Ay, what of that?

ACT IV, SCENE 1

The garden of the castle in Cyprus.

[OTHELLO and IAGO enter.]

IAGO   What do you think?

OTHELLO   Think about what, Iago?

IAGO   About kissing in private?

OTHELLO   A guilty kiss.

IAGO   Or to lie naked with her companion in bed innocently for an hour or more?

OTHELLO   Naked in bed, Iago, and still innocent? They put on the appearance of guilt when they are really innocent. By such actions, Satan tempts them as they tempt God.

IAGO   They commit no wrong. It is a forgivable error. But if I gave Emilia a handkerchief—

OTHELLO   What then?

IAGO   Then she owns it, sir. Because it is hers, she may give it to any man she chooses.

OTHELLO   She is the guardian of her honor as well. May she also give away her respectability?

IAGO   Honor is not visible. People who have lost honor often seem respectable. Back to the handkerchief—

OTHELLO   By God, I wish I could forget about the handkerchief! You said Cassio has my handkerchief. The loss sweeps over my mind like a crow stalking the dying.

IAGO   Is it important to you?

TRANSLATION

OTHELLO	That's not so good now.

IAGO
                                          What
If I had said I had seen him do you wrong?
Or heard him say—as knaves be such abroad   25
Who having, by their own importunate suit,
Or voluntary dotage of some mistress,
Convinced or supplied them, cannot choose
But they must blab—

OTHELLO   Hath he said anything?

IAGO He hath, my lord; but be you well assured,   30
No more than he'll unswear.

OTHELLO   What hath he said?

IAGO Faith, that he did—I know not what he did.

OTHELLO What? what?

IAGO Lie—

OTHELLO With her?   35

IAGO   With her, on her; what you will.

OTHELLO Lie with her? lie on her?—We say lie on
her when they belie her.—Lie with her! Zounds,
that's fulsome.—Handkerchief—confessions—
handkerchief!—To confess, and be hanged for his
labor—first to be hanged, and then to confess! I   40
tremble at it. Nature would not invest herself in such
shadowing passion without some instruction. It is
not words that shakes me thus.—Pish! Noses, ears,
and lips? Is't possible?—Confess?—Handkerchief?—O devil!
[Falls in a trance]

OTHELLO	It isn't good.
IAGO	Would it bother you if I reported his wrongdoings? Or if I heard him say, as rascals do when they tattle on their pursuit of a woman or of their fascination with a mistress.
OTHELLO	Has Cassio said anything about Desdemona?
IAGO	He has, sir, but you can be sure he will deny it.
OTHELLO	What did Cassio say?
IAGO	He said that he—I don't know what he did.
OTHELLO	What, what?
IAGO	He did lie.
OTHELLO	With Desdemona?
IAGO	With her, on her, *et cetera*.
OTHELLO	He lay with her? on her? To lie on her means that he gives a bad impression of her. Lie with Desdemona! God's wounds, that's too much to tolerate. The handkerchief, Cassio's gossip, the handkerchief! He confesses his evil and will be executed for his wickedness—first let him be hanged, then let him confess! The thought scares me. Nature should not cover me with a dark emotion without telling me how to manage it. I'm not afraid of words. Pish! Noses, ears, and lips? Could it be true? Did Cassio confess? Did Desdemona give up the handkerchief? Cassio is a demon! *[OTHELLO sinks into deep thought.]*

ACT IV

TRANSLATION

IAGO	Work on,	45
	My med'cine, work! Thus credulous fools are caught,	
	And many worthy and chaste dames even thus,	
	All guiltless, meet reproach.—What, ho! my lord!	
	My lord, I say! Othello!	
	[Enter CASSIO]	
	How now, Cassio?	
CASSIO	What's the matter?	50
IAGO	My lord is fall'n into an epilepsy.	
	This is his second fit; he had one yesterday.	
CASSIO	Rub him about the temples.	
IAGO	No, forbear.	
	The lethargy must have his quiet course.	
	If not, he foams at mouth, and by and by	55
	Breaks out to savage madness. Look, he stirs.	
	Do you withdraw yourself a little while.	
	He will recover straight. When he is gone,	
	I would on great occasion speak with you.	
	[Exit CASSIO]	
	How is it, general? Have you not hurt your head?	60
OTHELLO	Dost thou mock me?	
IAGO	I mock you? No, by heaven.	
	Would you would bear your fortune like a man!	
OTHELLO	A horned man's a monster and a beast.	
IAGO	There's many a beast then in a populous city,	
	And many a civil monster.	65
OTHELLO	Did he confess it?	
IAGO	Good sir, be a man.	
	Think every bearded fellow that's but yoked	
	May draw with you. There's millions now alive	
	That nightly lie in those unproper beds	
	Which they dare swear peculiar: your case is better.	70
	O, 'tis the spite of hell, the fiend's arch-mock,	
	To lip a wanton in a secure couch,	
	And to suppose her chaste! No, let me know;	
	And knowing what I am, I know what she shall be.	

ORIGINAL

IAGO	Continue to corrupt him, my trickery! This is the way to deceive naive fools. Many decent, pure wives encounter a charge of guilt. Sir, are you okay? Othello! Speak up! *[CASSIO enters.]* How are you, Cassio?
CASSIO	What is troubling Othello?
IAGO	The general has lapsed into a seizure. This is the second time. He had a seizure yesterday.
CASSIO	Massage his temples.
IAGO	No, don't. The sickness must pass quietly. If you disturb him, he dribbles saliva and eventually erupts in dangerous insanity. See, he is rousing. Stand aside for a while. He will soon be normal again. When he departs, I have something urgent to discuss with you. *[CASSIO goes out.]* How do you feel, General? Have you had a head injury?
OTHELLO	Are you making fun of me?
IAGO	Would I laugh at you? Never, by God. I want you to bear bad luck like a man!
OTHELLO	A betrayed husband becomes a monster, a beast.
IAGO	Every city contains betrayed husbands who control their beastliness.
OTHELLO	Did Cassio confess to adultery?
IAGO	Sir, get hold of yourself. Every betrayed man shares your burden. There are millions of betrayed men who share beds with adulterous wives without realizing the women's sin. Your situation is better. It is the devil's trick, to place a tart in a marriage bed and to pretend she is pure! As a husband, I want to know the truth about an adulterous wife.

ACT IV

TRANSLATION

OTHELLO	O, thou art wise! 'Tis certain. 75
IAGO	Stand you awhile apart;

IAGO   Stand you awhile apart;
Confine yourself but in a patient list.
Whilst you were here, o'erwhelmed with your grief—
A passion most unsuiting such a man—
Cassio came hither. I shifted him away
And laid good 'scuse upon your ecstasy: 80
Bade him anon return, and here speak with me;
The which he promised. Do but encave yourself
And mark the fleers, the gibes, and notable scorns
That dwell in every region of his face;
For I will make him tell the tale anew—   85
Where, how, how oft, how long ago, and when
He hath, and is again to cope your wife.
I say, but mark his gesture. Marry, patience!
Or I shall say you are all in all in spleen,
And nothing of a man.   90

OTHELLO   Dost thou hear, Iago?
I will be found most cunning in my patience;
But—dost thou hear?—most bloody.

IAGO   That's not amiss;
But yet keep time in all. Will you withdraw?
[OTHELLO retires]
Now will I question Cassio of Bianca,
A huswife that by selling her desires   95
Buys herself bread and clothes. It is a creature
That dotes on Cassio, as 'tis the strumpet's plague
To beguile many and be beguiled by one.
He, when he hears of her, cannot refrain
From the excess of laughter. Here he comes.   100
[Enter CASSIO]
As he shall smile, Othello shall go mad;
And his unbookish jealousy must conster
Poor Cassio's smiles, gestures, and light behavior
Quite in the wrong. How do you now, lieutenant?

CASSIO The worser that you give me the addition   105
Whose want even kills me.

OTHELLO	You are wise to prefer the truth about deception.
IAGO	Keep to yourself for a while. Be patient. While you swooned in grief, a terrible emotion for a man, Cassio approached. I sent him away and made excuses for your collapse. I told him to return later to talk with me. He promised to come back. Withdraw from Cassio's sight and observe the contempt, retorts, and scorn that dominate his face. I will ask him to tell me again about the affair with Desdemona. Where they go, how, how often, for how long, and when he has been with Desdemona and when they will meet again. Observe his gestures. Be patient! If you don't control your anger, you have lost your manhood.
OTHELLO	Hear this, Iago. I will be sneaky in my patience. But, hear this, I will be deadly.
IAGO	I would expect anger. Don't rush matters. Go hide from Cassio. *[OTHELLO withdraws from sight.]* I will ask Cassio about Bianca, a prostitute who sells her body to pay for her upkeep. She adores Cassio. It is the whore's fault to tempt many and love only one man. When he hears her name, he always laughs. Here he comes. *[CASSIO enters.]* When Cassio smiles, Othello will rage. Othello's ignorant suspicion will interpret Cassio's smiles, gestures, and happy behavior the wrong way. How are you, Lieutenant Cassio?
CASSIO	I feel worse when you call me lieutenant, a title I no longer hold.

ACT IV

TRANSLATION

IAGO	Ply Desdemona well, and you are sure on't. Now, if this suit lay in Bianca's power, How quickly should you speed!
CASSIO	Alas, poor caitiff!
OTHELLO	Look how he laughs already! 110
IAGO	I never knew a woman love man so.
CASSIO	Alas, poor rogue! I think, I' faith, she loves me.
OTHELLO	Now he denies it faintly, and laughs it out.
IAGO	Do you hear, Cassio?
OTHELLO	Now he importunes him To tell it o'er. Go to! Well said, well said! 115
IAGO	She gives it out that you shall marry her. Do you intend it?
CASSIO	Ha, ha, ha!
OTHELLO	Do you triumph, Roman? Do you triumph?
CASSIO	I marry her? What, a customer? Prithee 120 bear some charity to my wit; do not think it so unwholesome. Ha, ha, ha!
OTHELLO	So, so, so, so! They laugh that win!
IAGO	Faith, the cry goes that you shall marry her.
CASSIO	Prithee say true. 125
IAGO	I am a very villain else.
OTHELLO	Have you scored me? Well.
CASSIO	This is the monkey's own giving out. She is persuaded I will marry her out of her own love and flattery, not out of my promise. 130
OTHELLO	Iago beckons me; now he begins the story.
CASSIO	She was here even now; she haunts me in every place. I was t' other day talking on the sea bank with certain Venetians, and thither comes the bauble, and, by this hand, she falls me thus about 135 my neck—

ORIGINAL

IAGO	Beg Desdemona and you will get your title back. If you could beg Bianca for the title, you would get your post back even faster!
CASSIO	Alas that Bianca is a poor nobody!
OTHELLO	Look at Cassio laughing!
IAGO	I never saw a woman so in love with a man.
CASSIO	Alas, she's a character! I truly believe she loves me.
OTHELLO	He hesitates to deny her love for him and laughs about it.
IAGO	Have you heard, Cassio?
OTHELLO	Iago wheedles Cassio into admitting the affair. Good job! Well done.
IAGO	Bianca tells people that you will marry her. Do you plan to marry her?
CASSIO	Ha, ha, ha!
OTHELLO	Are you a valiant Roman? Do you deserve a victory parade?
CASSIO	You think I would marry her? Marry a prostitute? Please, give me credit for being smarter than that. Don't think me so witless. Ha, ha, ha!
OTHELLO	So! Cassio laughs because he has seduced Desdemona!
IAGO	Truly, rumor has it that you will marry her.
CASSIO	Are you telling the truth?
IAGO	I am a rogue if I lie.
OTHELLO	Have you scored a point against me? Well.
CASSIO	This is what Bianca says. She believes I will marry her because she loves and flatters me. I haven't promised anything.
OTHELLO	Iago is gesturing toward me. Cassio is telling his side of the affair with Desdemona.
CASSIO	Bianca was just here. She follows me everywhere. I was chatting on the shore with some Venetians the other day. Here comes Bianca and, I vow, she hugged me around the neck.

ACT IV

TRANSLATION

OTHELLO	Crying 'O dear Cassio!' as it were. His gesture imports it.
CASSIO	So hangs, and lolls, and weeps upon me; so hales and pulls me! Ha, ha, ha! 140
OTHELLO	Now he tells how she plucked him to my chamber. O, I see that nose of yours, but not that dog I shall throw't to.
CASSIO	Well, I must leave her company. *[Enter BIANCA]*
IAGO	Before me! Look where she comes. 145
CASSIO	'Tis such another fitchew! marry, a perfumed one. What do you mean by this haunting of me?
BIANCA	Let the devil and his dam haunt you! What did you mean by that same handkerchief you gave me even now? I was a fine fool to take it. I 150 must take out the whole work? A likely piece of work that you should find it in your chamber and know not who left it there! This is some minx's token, and I must take out the work? There! Give it your hobby-horse. Wheresoever you had it, I'll 155 take out no work on't.
CASSIO	How now, my sweet Bianca? How now? how now?
OTHELLO	By heaven, that should be my handkerchief!
BIANCA	An you'll come to supper to-night, you may; an you will not, come when you are next prepared for. 160 *[Exit]*
IAGO	After her, after her!
CASSIO	Faith, I must; she'll rail i' th' street else.
IAGO	Will you sup there?
CASSIO	Yes, I intend so.
IAGO	Well, I may chance to see you; for I would 165 very fain speak with you.
CASSIO	Prithee come. Will you?
IAGO	Go to! say no more. *[Exit CASSIO]*

OTHELLO	Proclaiming "Dear Cassio!" His gesture implies a public display of affection.
CASSIO	She pulls at me and snuggles and cries over me. She calls me and pulls at me! Ha, ha, ha!
OTHELLO	Now Cassio describes how Desdemona dragged him to my bedroom. I see your nose, but I don't see the hound that I shall toss it to.
CASSIO	I must give up pursuing Bianca. *[BIANCA enters.]*
IAGO	I declare, here she comes now.
CASSIO	She's a skunk, one wearing perfume. Why are you following me?
BIANCA	Let Satan and his wife follow you! What did you mean by giving me this handkerchief? I was foolish to accept it. You want me to copy the embroidery? I doubt that you found the handkerchief in your room without knowing who left it there! This is some sweetie's gift and you want me to copy it? Here, give it back to your playmate. Wherever you got the handkerchief, I won't copy it.
CASSIO	Why, sweet Bianca? What's the matter?
OTHELLO	By God, I should have that handkerchief!
BIANCA	If you want dinner tonight, then come visit. If you don't want dinner with me, don't expect me to cook for you again. *[BIANCA goes out.]*
IAGO	Go after her, Cassio.
CASSIO	I must stop her. She will complain in public if I don't.
IAGO	Will you dine with her?
CASSIO	Yes, I plan to.
IAGO	I may join you there. I need to talk to you.
CASSIO	Yes, join me, please.
IAGO	Please, say no more. *[CASSIO goes out.]*

ACT IV

TRANSLATION

OTHELLO	*[Comes forward]* How shall I murder him, Iago?
IAGO	Did you perceive how he laughed at his vice? 170
OTHELLO	O Iago!
IAGO	And did you see the handkerchief?
OTHELLO	Was that mine?
IAGO	Yours, by this hand! And to see how he prizes the foolish woman your wife! She gave it him, and 175 he hath giv'n it his whore.
OTHELLO	I would have him nine years a-killing!— A fine woman! a fair woman! a sweet woman!
IAGO	Nay, you must forget that.
OTHELLO	Ay, let her rot, and perish, and be damned 180 to-night; for she shall not live. No, my heart is turned to stone; I strike it, and it hurts my hand. O, the world hath not a sweeter creature! She might lie by an emperor's side and command him tasks.
IAGO	Nay, that's not your way. 185
OTHELLO	Hang her! I do but say what she is. So delicate with her needle! an admirable musician! O, she will sing the savageness out of a bear! Of so high and plenteous wit and invention—
IAGO	She's the worse for all this. 190
OTHELLO	O, a thousand thousand times! And then, of so gentle a condition!
IAGO	Ay, too gentle.
OTHELLO	Nay, that's certain. But yet the pity of it, Iago! O Iago, the pity of it, Iago! 195
IAGO	If you are so fond over her iniquity, give her patent to offend; for if it touch not you, it comes near nobody.
OTHELLO	I will chop her into messes! Cuckold me!
IAGO	O, 'tis foul in her.
OTHELLO	With mine officer! 200

OTHELLO	*[OTHELLO comes out of hiding.]* How shall I kill him, Iago.
IAGO	Did you notice how he laughed at his adultery?
OTHELLO	Oh, Iago!
IAGO	Did you spy the handkerchief?
OTHELLO	Was it the one I gave Desdemona?
IAGO	It was, I swear! And you should see how he values your silly wife. Desdemona gave the handkerchief to Cassio and he gave it to his prostitute.
OTHELLO	I would stretch his death over nine years! Oh what a fine lady, a pretty lady, a sweet lady!
IAGO	Don't obsess over her crimes.
OTHELLO	Yes, let her rot and die and go to hell tonight, for I will kill her. My heart is hard. I pound on it and bruise my hand. Oh, there's no sweeter woman in the world! She could be an emperor's love and assign him chores.
IAGO	This is not how you should behave.
OTHELLO	May she hang! I am only telling the truth. So delicate a seamstress, so talented a musician! She could sing the growl out of a bear! She has such generous wit and good humor.
IAGO	For all these qualities, she seems even worse.
OTHELLO	She is a thousand times worse! And she acts so sweet!
IAGO	Yes, too sweet.
OTHELLO	That's for sure. Oh, the pity of her wickedness, Iago. Oh, Iago, the pity of her wickedness, Iago.
IAGO	If you love her even though she is bad, let her continue her evil life. If you can tolerate it, it won't hurt anyone else.
OTHELLO	I will hack her to pieces! How dare she betray me!
IAGO	It is a foul crime.
OTHELLO	With my own officer!

ACT IV

IAGO	That's fouler.
OTHELLO	Get me some poison, Iago, this night. I'll not expostulate with her, lest her body and beauty unprovide my mind again. This night, Iago!
IAGO	Do it not with poison. Strangle her in her 205 bed, even the bed she hath contaminated.
OTHELLO	Good, good! The justice of it pleases. Very good!
IAGO	And for Cassio, let me be his undertaker: you shall hear more by midnight.
OTHELLO	Excellent good! 210 *[A trumpet]* What trumpet is that same?
IAGO	Something from Venice, sure. *[Enter LODOVICO, DESDEMONA, and Attendants]* 'Tis Lodovico Come from the Duke; and see, your wife is with him.
LODOVICO	God save you, worthy general!
OTHELLO	With all my heart, sir.
LODOVICO	The Duke and senators of Venice greet you. 215 *[Gives him a letter]*
OTHELLO	I kiss the instrument of their pleasures. *[Opens the letter and reads]*
DESDEMONA	And what's the news, good cousin Lodovico?
IAGO	I am very glad to see you, signior. Welcome to Cyprus.
LODOVICO	I thank you. How does Lieutenant Cassio? 220
IAGO	Lives, sir.
DESDEMONA	Cousin, there's fall'n between him and my lord An unkind breach; but you shall make all well.
OTHELLO	Are you sure of that?
DESDEMONA	My lord?
OTHELLO	*[Reads]* 'This fail you not to do, as you will—,' 225

IAGO	That's even worse.
OTHELLO	Bring me some poison tonight, Iago. I won't accuse her because her form and beauty may change my mind. Bring it tonight, Iago!
IAGO	Don't poison her. Strangle her in the bed she shared with Cassio.
OTHELLO	Good idea. That's an appropriate place for her to die. Very good!
IAGO	Let me be the one to haul out Cassio's carcass. I will return to you by midnight.
OTHELLO	Very good! *[A trumpet sounds.]* What is that trumpet call?
IAGO	It must be a message from Venice. *[LODOVICO, DESDE-MONA, and attendants enter.]* It's Lodovico, the Duke's messenger. See, Desdemona accompanies him.
LODOVICO	God save you, worthy General Othello!
OTHELLO	I heartily thank you, sir.
LODOVICO	The Duke and senators of Venice send you greetings. *[LODOVICO gives OTHELLO a letter from the Duke.]*
OTHELLO	I welcome this letter. *[OTHELLO opens the letter and reads it.]*
DESDEMONA	Do you bring news, cousin Lodovico?
IAGO	I am happy to see you, sir. Welcome to Cyprus.
LODOVICO	Thank you. How is Lieutenant Cassio?
IAGO	He survived the war, sir.
DESDEMONA	Othello and Cassio have had a quarrel, Lodovico, but you will repair their friendship.
OTHELLO	Are you certain, Desdemona?
DESDEMONA	My lord?
OTHELLO	*[OTHELLO reads aloud.]* "You must not fail your duty—"

ACT IV

TRANSLATION

LODOVICO	He did not call; he's busy in the paper.
	Is there division 'twixt thy lord and Cassio?
DESDEMONA	A most unhappy one. I would do much
	T' atone them, for the love I bear to Cassio.
OTHELLO	Fire and brimstone! 230
DESDEMONA	My lord?
OTHELLO	Are you wise?
DESDEMONA	What, is he angry?
LODOVICO	Maybe the letter moved him;
	For, as I think, they do command him home,
	Deputing Cassio in his government.
DESDEMONA	By my troth, I am glad on't.
OTHELLO	Indeed?
DESDEMONA	My lord?
OTHELLO	I am glad to see you mad. 235
DESDEMONA	Why, sweet Othello—
OTHELLO	Devil!
	[Strikes her]
DESDEMONA	I have not deserved this.
LODOVICO	My lord, this would not be believed in Venice,
	Though I should swear I saw't. 'Tis very much.
	Make her amends; she weeps. 240
OTHELLO	O devil, devil!
	If that the earth could teem with woman's tears,
	Each drop she falls would prove a crocodile.
	Out of my sight!
DESDEMONA	I will not stay to offend you.
	[Going]
LODOVICO	Truly, an obedient lady. 245
	I do beseech your lordship call her back.

LODOVICO	He wasn't talking to you. He's reading the letter. Is there a squabble between Othello and Cassio?
DESDEMONA	A bad one. I would do anything to reconcile them for my love for Cassio.
OTHELLO	Fire and sulfur!
DESDEMONA	My lord?
OTHELLO	Are you thinking clearly?
DESDEMONA	Why is Othello angry?
LODOVICO	Maybe something in the letter disturbed him. I think the Duke orders Othello back to Venice and appoints Cassio as governor of Cyprus.
DESDEMONA	Truly, I am happy to hear it.
OTHELLO	Really?
DESDEMONA	My lord?
OTHELLO	I am glad to see you angry.
DESDEMONA	Why, gentle Othello—
OTHELLO	Demon! *[OTHELLO strikes DESDEMONA.]*
DESDEMONA	I don't deserve punishment.
LODOVICO	Sir, nobody in Venice will believe you hit her, even if I swear I saw it happen. This is terrible. Apologize. She is crying.
OTHELLO	Oh, you demon! If the earth should grow fruitful from women's tears, each drop would produce a crocodile. Get out of my sight!
DESDEMONA	I will not continue to upset you. *[DESDEMONA, turning to go.]*
LODOVICO	She is obedient, Othello. I urge you to call her back.

ACT IV

TRANSLATION

OTHELLO	Mistress!
DESDEMONA	My lord?
OTHELLO	What would you with her, sir?
LODOVICO	Who? I, my lord?
OTHELLO	Ay! You did wish that I would make her turn.
	Sir, she can turn, and turn, and yet go on 250
	And turn again; and she can weep, sir, weep;
	And she's obedient; as you say, obedient,
	Very obedient.—Proceed you in your tears.—
	Concerning this, sir—O well-painted passion!—
	I am commanded home.—Get you away; 255
	I'll send for you anon.—Sir, I obey the mandate
	And will return to Venice.—Hence, avaunt!
	[Exit DESDEMONA]
	Cassio shall have my place, And, sir, to-night
	I do entreat that we may sup together.
	You are welcome, sir, to Cyprus.—Goats and monkeys! 260
	[Exit]
LODOVICO	Is this the noble Moor whom our full Senate
	Call all in all sufficient? Is this the nature
	Whom passion could not shake? whose solid virtue
	The shot of accident nor dart of chance
	Could neither graze nor pierce? 265
IAGO	He is much changed.
LODOVICO	Are his wits safe? Is he not light of brain?
IAGO	He's that he is; I may not breathe my censure.
	What he might be—if what he might he is not—
	I would to heaven he were!
LODOVICO	What, strike his wife?
IAGO	Faith, that was not so well; yet would I knew 270
	That stroke would prove the worst!
LODOVICO	Is it his use?
	Or did the letters work upon his blood
	And new-create this fault?

OTHELLO	Wife!
DESDEMONA	My lord?
OTHELLO	What do you want me to say to her, Lodovico?
LODOVICO	I, my lord? What would I say to her?
OTHELLO	Yes. You asked me to call her back. She is good at turning again and again. And she is talented at tears. And she obeys me, as you see, she is quite obedient. Go on and cry. Concerning this letter, Lodovico—She conceals her passion well! The Duke orders me home. Go away, Desdemona. I will call for you later. Sir, I will obey the order and return to Venice. Go, at once! *[DESDEMONA exits.]* Cassio will take my place here on Cyprus. And Lodovico, I invite you to dinner tonight. I welcome you to Cyprus, sir. Lustful goats and monkeys! *[OTHELLO goes out.]*
LODOVICO	Is Othello the very man whom the Senate calls sane? Is this the man who controls his emotions? Is this the man whose goodness is unharmed by accident or luck?
IAGO	He has changed a great deal.
LODOVICO	Is he sane? Is he not unbalanced?
IAGO	He is what he's always been. I don't dare criticize him. I wish God would make Othello what he should be.
LODOVICO	Dared he hit his wife?
IAGO	That was bad. I wish that were the worst Othello could behave!
LODOVICO	Is this his usual behavior? Did the letter upset him and revive an old fault?

ACT IV

TRANSLATION

IAGO   Alas, alas!
It is not honesty in me to speak
What I have seen and known. You shall observe him,   275
And his own courses will denote him so
That I may save my speech. Do but go after
And mark how he continues.

LODOVICO   I am sorry that I am deceived in him.
[Exeunt]

IAGO	I should not report what I haven't seen or learned first-hand. You shall observe his actions. I will let his actions speak for themselves. Follow him and watch how he behaves.
LODOVICO	I am sorry for having the wrong opinion of Othello. *[LODOVICO and IAGO go out.]*

TRANSLATION

ACT IV, SCENE 2

A room in the castle.

[Enter OTHELLO and EMILIA]

OTHELLO	You have seen nothing then?	
EMILIA	Nor ever heard, nor ever did suspect.	
OTHELLO	Yes, you have seen Cassio and she together.	
EMILIA	But then I saw no harm, and then I heard	
	Each syllable that breath made up between them.	5
OTHELLO	What, did they never whisper?	
EMILIA	Never, my lord.	
OTHELLO	Nor send you out o'th' way?	
EMILIA	Never.	
OTHELLO	To fetch her fan, her gloves, her mask, nor nothing?	
EMILIA	Never, my lord.	10
OTHELLO	That's strange.	

EMILIA   I durst, my lord, to wager she is honest,
Lay down my soul at stake. If you think other,
Remove your thought; it doth abuse your bosom.
If any wretch have put this in your head,   15
Let heaven requite it with the serpent's curse!
For if she be not honest, chaste, and true,
There's no man happy; the purest of their wives
Is foul as slander.

OTHELLO   Bid her come hither. Go.
[Exit EMILIA]
She says enough; yet she's a simple bawd   20
That cannot say as much. This is a subtle whore,
A closet lock and key of villainous secrets;
And yet she'll kneel and pray; I have seen her do't.
[Enter DESDEMONA and EMILIA]

ACT IV, SCENE 2

A room in the castle at Cyprus.

[OTHELLO and EMILIA enter.]

OTHELLO	Have you witnessed nothing wrong?
EMILIA	I have heard nothing and suspected nothing wrong.
OTHELLO	You have seen her with Cassio.
EMILIA	I have seen nothing but conversation, which I heard in its entirety.
OTHELLO	They don't ever whisper?
EMILIA	Never, sir.
OTHELLO	They never send you away?
EMILIA	Never.
OTHELLO	Not to get her fan, her gloves, her face covering, nothing?
EMILIA	Never, sir.
OTHELLO	That's odd.
EMILIA	I would bet my soul, sir, that she is faithful to you. If you suspect otherwise, wipe that thought from your mind. Such a suspicion troubles your heart. If any villain put this thought in your mind, let God curse him like the snake in the Garden of Eden! If Desdemona is not honest, pure, and faithful, then no man is lucky. The purest of their wives is corrupt as lies.
OTHELLO	Tell her to come here. Go. *[EMILIA goes out.]* Emilia says the right thing, yet, any madam can lie for a whore. This is a crafty prostitute who locks away evil secrets. And yet, she pretends to kneel and pray. I have watched her. *[DESDEMONA and EMILIA enter.]*

ACT IV

TRANSLATION

DESDEMONA	My lord, what is your will?
OTHELLO	Pray, chuck, come hither.
DESDEMONA	What is your pleasure? 25
OTHELLO	Let me see your eyes. Look in my face.
DESDEMONA	What horrible fancy's this?
OTHELLO	*[To EMILIA]* Some of your function, mistress. Leave procreants alone and shut the door; Cough or cry hem if anybody come. Your mystery, your mystery! Nay, dispatch! 30 *[Exit EMILIA]*
DESDEMONA	Upon my knees, what doth your speech import? I understand a fury in your words, But not the words.
OTHELLO	Why, what art thou?
DESDEMONA	Your wife, my lord; your true And loyal wife. 35
OTHELLO	Come, swear it, damn thyself; Lest, being like one of heaven, the devils themselves Should fear to seize thee. Therefore be double-damned— Swear thou art honest.
DESDEMONA	Heaven doth truly know it.
OTHELLO	Heaven truly knows that thou art false as hell.
DESDEMONA	To whom, my lord? With whom? How am I false? 40
OTHELLO	Ah, Desdemon! Away! away! away!
DESDEMONA	Alas the heavy day! Why do you weep? Am I the motive of these tears, my lord? If haply you my father do suspect An instrument of this your calling back, 45 Lay not your blame on me. If you have lost him, Why, I have lost him too.

ORIGINAL

DESDEMONA	Sir, did you want something?
OTHELLO	Pray, sweetheart, come here.
DESDEMONA	What can I do for you.
OTHELLO	I want to see your eyes. Look at my face.
DESDEMONA	What terrible imagination caused you to ask?
OTHELLO	*[OTHELLO speaks to EMILIA.]* This is your job, Emilia. Leave lovers in private and close the door. Cough or make a warning sound if anybody approaches. It's your job! Go, hurry! *[EMILIA goes out.]*
DESDEMONA	I beg of you, what do mean by this talk? I hear anger in your words, but I don't understand your meaning.
OTHELLO	What are you?
DESDEMONA	I am your wife, sir, your honest and faithful wife.
OTHELLO	Damn your soul by swearing your loyalty. By pretending to be an angel, you scare off the demons themselves. Double-doom yourself—pledge your loyalty.
DESDEMONA	God knows that I am faithful.
OTHELLO	God knows that you are evil as hell.
DESDEMONA	To whom, sir? With whom? How have I been dishonest?
OTHELLO	Desdemona! Go away!
DESDEMONA	What a sad day! Why are you crying? Have I caused your distress, sir? If you suspect my father Brabantio of having you called back to Venice, don't blame me. If he has turned against you, he has also discharged me.

ACT IV

TRANSLATION

OTHELLO	Had it pleased heaven
	To try me with affliction, had they rained
	All kinds of sores and shames on my bare head,
	Steeped me in poverty to the very lips,
	Given to captivity me and my utmost hopes,
	I should have found in some place of my soul
	A drop of patience. But, alas, to make me
	A fixed figure for the time of scorn
	To point his slow unmoving finger at!
	Yet could I bear that too; well, very well,
	But there where I have garnered up my heart,
	Where either I must live or bear no life;
	The fountain from the which my current runs
	Or else dries up—to be discarded thence,
	Or keep it as a cistern for foul toads
	To knot and gender in—turn thy complexion there,
	Patience, thou young and rose-lipped cherubin!
	Ay, there look grim as hell!

Line numbers (right margin): 50, 55, 60

DESDEMONA I hope my noble lord esteems me honest. 65

OTHELLO
O, ay; as summer flies are in the shambles,
That quicken even with blowing, O thou weed,
Who art so lovely fair, and smell'st so sweet,
That the sense aches at thee, would thou had'st ne'er
    been born!

DESDEMONA Alas, what ignorant sin have I committed? 70

OTHELLO
Was this fair paper, this most goodly book,
Made to write 'whore' upon? What committed?
Committed? O thou public commoner!
I should make very forges of my cheeks
That would to cinders burn up modesty, 75
Did I but speak thy deeds. What committed?
Heaven stops the nose at it, and the moon winks;
The bawdy wind, that kisses all it meets,
Is hushed within the hollow mine of earth
And will not hear it. What committed? 80
Impudent strumpet!

OTHELLO	If God were testing me with woes, if they fell like sores and humiliations on me, dipped me in poverty up to the mouth, imprisoned me and my ambition, I would find a bit of patience in my soul. But to scorn me, to point God's unshakable finger at! I could tolerate that punishment well. But God wounds me in the heart, where I must live or die. The source from which my blood flows or dries up. My heart should be discarded or kept as a well for toads to copulate in. Let patience, a young angel, end there! At that point, patience looks grim as hell!
DESDEMONA	I hope my lord trusts me.
OTHELLO	Yes, as summer flies spring to life in a slaughterhouse. You weed who look so pretty and smell so sweet that you make my senses ache, I wish you had never been born.
DESDEMONA	What sin have I committed that I don't know of?
OTHELLO	Was this clean paper, this clear page, meant for me to write "whore" on it? What have you done? Done? Oh, streetwalker! I would turn my cheeks red by burning your modesty to ash if I described your sins. What have you done? God holds his nose at your shame and the moon shuts his eyes. The loose wind that embraces everything hides in the center of the earth and will not listen to your confession. What have you done? Sassy whore!

ACT IV

DESDEMONA	By heaven, you do me wrong!
OTHELLO	Are not you a strumpet?
DESDEMONA	No, as I am a Christian!
	If to preserve this vessel for my lord
	From any other foul unlawful touch
	Be not to be a strumpet, I am none.

85

OTHELLO	What, not a whore?
DESDEMONA	No, as I shall be saved!
OTHELLO	Is't possible?
DESDEMONA	O, heaven forgive us!
OTHELLO	I cry you mercy then.
	I took you for that cunning whore of Venice
	That married with Othello—*[Calling]* You, mistress,
	That have the office opposite to Saint Peter
	And keep the gate of hell!
	[Enter EMILIA]
	You, you, ay, you!
	We have done our course; there's money for your pains:
	I pray you turn the key, and keep our counsel.
	[Exit]

90

EMILIA	Alas, what does this gentleman conceive?
	How do you, madam? How do you, my good lady?
DESDEMONA	Faith, half asleep.
EMILIA	Good madam, what's the matter with my lord?
DESDEMONA	With who?
EMILIA	Why, with my lord, madam.
DESDEMONA	Who is thy lord?
EMILIA	He that is yours, sweet lady.
DESDEMONA	I have none. Do not talk to me, Emilia.
	I cannot weep; nor answer have I none
	But what should go by water. Prithee to-night
	Lay on my bed my wedding sheets, remember;
	And call thy husband hither.

95

100

105

DESDEMONA	By God, you are wrong!
OTHELLO	Are you not a prostitute?
DESDEMONA	No, on my honor as a Christian! If to guard my body for my husband from any lustful hand proves me not a whore, then I am pure.
OTHELLO	What, not a prostitute?
DESDEMONA	No, on my soul's salvation!
OTHELLO	Can it be possible?
DESDEMONA	God forgive us!
OTHELLO	I grant you mercy. I thought you were the crafty prostitute of Venice that wed Othello. *[Calling to EMILIA]* You, Emilia, that is gatekeeper of hell as Saint Peter keeps the entrance to heaven! *[EMILIA enters.]* You, yes, you! We have completed our business. Here is your fee. Please unlock the door and keep our secret. *[OTHELLO goes out.]*
EMILIA	What does Othello imagine? Are you all right, madam? Are you all right, good Desdemona?
DESDEMONA	I must be dreaming.
EMILIA	Madam, what is wrong with Othello?
DESDEMONA	With whom?
EMILIA	With my lord, madam.
DESDEMONA	Who is your lord?
EMILIA	He is your husband, lady.
DESDEMONA	I have no husband. Be silent, Emilia. I can't cry, I can't reply anything but something to make me weep. Please, put my wedding sheets on my bed and summon Iago.

ACT IV

TRANSLATION

EMILIA	Here's a change indeed!
	[Exit]
DESDEMONA	'Tis meet I should be used so, very meet.
	How have I been behaved, that he might stick
	The small'st opinion on my least misuse?
	[Enter IAGO and EMILIA]
IAGO	What is your pleasure, madam? How is't with you? 110
DESDEMONA	I cannot tell. Those that do teach young babes
	Do it with gentle means and easy tasks:
	He might have chid me so; for, in good faith,
	I am a child to chiding.
IAGO	What is the matter, lady?
EMILIA	Alas, Iago, my lord hath so bewhored her, 115
	Thrown such despite and heavy terms upon her
	As true hearts cannot bear.
DESDEMONA	Am I that name, Iago?
IAGO	What name, fair lady?
DESDEMONA	Such as she says my lord did say I was.
EMILIA	He called her whore. A beggar in his drink 120
	Could not have laid such terms upon his callet.
IAGO	Why did he so?
DESDEMONA	I do not know; I am sure I am none such.
IAGO	Do not weep, do not weep. Alas the day!
EMILIA	Hath she forsook so many noble matches, 125
	Her father and her country, all her friends,
	To be called whore? Would it not make one weep?
DESDEMONA	It is my wretched fortune.
IAGO	Beshrew him for't!
	How comes this trick upon him?
DESDEMONA	Nay, heaven doth know.
EMILIA	I will be hanged if some eternal villain, 130
	Some busy and insinuating rogue,
	Some cogging, cozening slave, to get some office,
	Have not devised this slander. I'll be hanged else.

EMILIA	This is a strange answer! *[EMILIA goes out.]*
DESDEMONA	It is not surprising that he should treat me like this. What have I done to make him suspect me of even a small fault? *[IAGO and EMILIA enter.]*
IAGO	What do you need, madam? Are you all right?
DESDEMONA	I don't know. People who teach babies do it gently by beginning with easy lessons. Othello might be scolding me the same way. Truly, I am not accustomed to scolding.
IAGO	What is wrong, ma'am?
EMILIA	Iago, Othello has so insulted her and hurled such cruel charges at her that good hearts can't bear it.
DESDEMONA	Am I what she said, Iago?
IAGO	What, good lady?
DESDEMONA	Am I what Emilia says that Othello called me?
EMILIA	He called her a prostitute. A drunk beggar could not have abased his woman so.
IAGO	Why did he do it?
DESDEMONA	I don't know. I am innocent.
IAGO	Don't cry. What a terrible day!
EMILIA	Did she refuse noble suitors and defy her father, Venice, and her friends to be called a whore? Would Othello's rage not make anybody cry?
DESDEMONA	It is a terrible destiny.
IAGO	Forgive him for it! Why has Othello turned into a scold?
DESDEMONA	Only God knows.
EMILIA	I am certain that some criminal, some lying rascal, some cheating, deceiving underling made up this lie to gain a promotion. I stake my life on it.

ACT IV

TRANSLATION

IAGO	Fie, there is no such man! It is impossible.
DESDEMONA	If any such there be, heaven pardon him! 135
EMILIA	A halter pardon him! and hell gnaw his bones!
	Why should he call her whore? Who keeps her company?
	What place? what time? what form? what likelihood?
	The Moor's abused by some most villainous knave,
	Some base notorious knave, some scurvy fellow. 140
	O heaven, that such companions thou'dst unfold,
	And put in every honest hand a whip
	To lash the rascals naked through the world
	Even from the east to th' west!
IAGO	Speak within door.
EMILIA	O, fie upon them! Some such squire he was 145
	That turned your wit the seamy side without
	And made you to suspect me with the Moor.
IAGO	You are a fool. Go to.
DESDEMONA	O good Iago,
	What shall I do to win my lord again?
	Good friend, go to him; for, by this light of heaven, 150
	I know not how I lost him. Here I kneel:
	If e'er my will did trespass 'gainst his love
	Either in discourse of thought or actual deed,
	Or that mine eyes, mine ears, or any sense
	Delighted them in any other form, 155
	Or that I do not yet, and ever did,
	And ever will (though he do shake me off
	To beggarly divorcement) love him dearly,
	Comfort forswear me! Unkindness may do much;
	And his unkindness may defeat my life, 160
	But never taint my love. I cannot say 'whore.'
	It doth abhor me now I speak the word;
	To do the act that might th' addition earn
	Not the world's mass of vanity could make me.
IAGO	I pray you be content. 'Tis but his humor. 165
	The business of the state does him offense,
	(And he does chide with you).

IAGO	Nonsense. There is no man so low. It is impossible.
DESDEMONA	If any villain be so bad, let God pardon him!
EMILIA	A noose should pardon him! and Satan chew his bones! Why should Othello call her a whore? Who courts her? Where, when, how, why? Some vile rogue, some low-life scum, some diseased person has tricked Othello. Oh, God, such wretches should be whipped naked by every honest person around the world, from east to west!
IAGO	Guard your accusations.
EMILIA	Oh, damn my words! Some disreputable man turned your thinking inside out and made Othello suspect me of lying.
IAGO	You are foolish. Nonsense.
DESDEMONA	Iago, how can I win Othello's trust again? Go find him. By God, I don't know how I betrayed him. I kneel to say, if I ever sinned against him in thought or action, If my eyes, ears, or senses admired any other man, if I didn't love him truly and always will, even if he divorces me, may I never be comforted. He may kill me with cruelty, but he can't corrupt my love for him. I cannot pronounce "whore"; I detest speaking the word. I couldn't be a strumpet for all the world's rewards.
IAGO	Don't worry. It is his mood. Business from Venice has upset him, and he took out his anger on you.

ACT IV

TRANSLATION

DESDEMONA	If 'twere no other—
IAGO	'Tis but so, I warrant.

[Trumpets within]
Hark how these instruments summon you to supper.
The messengers of Venice stay the meat: 170
Go in, and weep not. All things shall be well.
[Exeunt DESDEMONA and EMILIA]
[Enter RODERIGO]
How now, Roderigo?

RODERIGO	I do not find that thou deal'st justly with me.
IAGO	What in the contrary?

RODERIGO	Every day thou daff'st me with some device, 175

Iago, and rather, as it seems to me now, keep'st
from me all conveniency than suppliest me with the
least advantage of hope. I will indeed no longer
endure it; nor am I yet persuaded to put up in peace
what already I have foolishly suffered.   180

IAGO	Will you hear me, Roderigo?
RODERIGO	Faith, I have heard too much; for your

words and performance are no kin together.

IAGO	You charge me most unjustly.
RODERIGO	With naught but truth. I have wasted myself 185

out of means. The jewels you have had from me to
deliver to Desdemona would half have corrupted
a votarist. You have told me she hath received
them, and returned me expectations and comforts of
sudden respect and acquaintance; but I find none.   190

IAGO	Well, go to; very well.
RODERIGO	Very well! go to! I cannot go to, man;

nor 'tis not very well. By this hand, I say 'tis very
scurvy, and begin to find myself fopped in it.

IAGO	Very well. 195
RODERIGO	I tell you 'tis not very well. I will make

myself known to Desdemona. If she will return me
my jewels, I will give over my suit and repent my
unlawful solicitation; if not, assure yourself I will seek
satisfaction of you.   200

ORIGINAL

DESDEMONA	If that is all that is wrong with him—
IAGO	I promise, that is all. *[Trumpets sound in the castle.]* Trumpeters call you to dinner. The messengers from Venice await their meal. Go to dinner and don't cry. All will be well. *[DESDEMONA and EMILIA depart.]* *[RODERIGO enters.]* What is it, Roderigo?
RODERIGO	You have been unjust to me.
IAGO	I have been false?
RODERIGO	Every day, you make up some excuse, Iago. You keep me from any hope of having Desdemona. I can't stand the delay. I won't tolerate any more suffering.
IAGO	Listen to me, Roderigo.
RODERIGO	I have heard too much from you. You don't keep your word.
IAGO	You are wrong.
RODERIGO	It is true. I have spent my money. The jewelry I have bought for you to deliver to Desdemona would lure a nun. You told me she received my gifts and planned to reply, but she hasn't.
IAGO	All right. Be calm.
RODERIGO	All right! Be calm! I can't be calm, man. Nor is it all right. Your treatment is base. You have made a fool of me.
IAGO	All right.
RODERIGO	I tell you it isn't all right. I want to speak directly to Desdemona. If she will return the jewelry, I will stop courting her and repent of seeking a married woman. If she won't return them, I will take out my anger on you.

ACT IV

TRANSLATION

IAGO	You have said now.
RODERIGO	Ay, and said nothing but what I protest intendment of doing.
IAGO	Why, now I see there's mettle in thee; and even from this instant do build on thee a better opinion than ever before. Give me thy hand, Roderigo. Thou hast taken against me a most just exception; but yet I protest I have dealt most directly in thy affair.
RODERIGO	It hath not appeared.
IAGO	I grant indeed it hath not appeared, and your suspicion is not without wit and judgment. But, Roderigo, if thou hast that in thee indeed which I have greater reason to believe now than ever, I mean purpose, courage and valor, this night show it. If thou the next night following enjoy not Desdemona, take me from this world with treachery and devise engines for my life.
RODERIGO	Well, what is it? Is it within reason and compass?
IAGO	Sir, there is especial commission come from Venice to depute Cassio in Othello's place.
RODERIGO	Is that true? Why, then Othello and Desdemona return again to Venice.
IAGO	O, no; he goes into Mauritania and takes away with him the fair Desdemona, unless his abode be lingered here by some accident; wherein none can be so determinate as the removing of Cassio.
RODERIGO	How do you mean removing of him?
IAGO	Why, by making him uncapable of Othello's place—knocking out his brains.
RODERIGO	And that you would have me to do?

205

210

215

220

225

230

IAGO	That's enough.
RODERIGO	Yes, I have said what I intend to do.
IAGO	You have courage. You are a better man than I once thought. Shake hands, Roderigo. You are right to complain. I swear that I have done as I promised.
RODERIGO	It hasn't worked.
IAGO	It hasn't and you are wise to question me. If you have the aim, courage, and daring to win Desdemona, reveal it tonight. If the next night you aren't Desdemona's lover, then bring torments to kill me.
RODERIGO	What has happened? Do you have reason to say so?
IAGO	There is a delegation here from Venice to replace Othello with Cassio.
RODERIGO	Really? Then Othello and Desdemona are going back to Venice?
IAGO	No. Othello will move on to Mauritania in northwest Africa, unless there is some reason for him to delay here. Cassio must be removed.
RODERIGO	Why must he be removed?
IAGO	By killing him to keep him from replacing Othello.
RODERIGO	You want me to kill Cassio?

ACT IV

TRANSLATION

| IAGO | Ay, if you dare do yourself a profit and a right. He sups to-night with a harlotry, and thither will I go to him. He knows not yet of his honorable fortune. If you will watch his going thence, which I will fashion to fall out between twelve and one, you may take him at your pleasure. I will be near to second your attempt, and he shall fall between us. Come, stand not amazed at it, but go along with me. I will show you such a necessity in his death that you shall think yourself bound to put it on him. It is now high supper time, and the night grows to waste. About it! | 235 |

235

240

RODERIGO   I will hear further reason for this.

IAGO   And you shall be satisfied.   245
            [Exeunt]

IAGO	Yes, for your own good. I am joining him at dinner with his prostitute Bianca. He doesn't know he's been promoted. If you watch for his departure between midnight and 1:00 a.m., you can easily overpower him. I will follow him and help you murder him. Don't look so surprised. Come with me. I will explain why he must die. You will be convinced. It is nearly dinner time and the night is wasting. Let's go!
RODERIGO	You haven't convinced me.
IAGO	I will. *[IAGO and RODERIGO depart.]*

ACT IV, SCENE 3

Another room in the castle.

[Enter OTHELLO, LODOVICO, DESDEMONA, EMILIA, and Attendants]

LODOVICO   I do beseech you, Sir, trouble yourself no further.

OTHELLO   O, pardon me; 'twill do me good to walk.

LODOVICO   Madam, good night. I humbly thank your ladyship.

DESDEMONA   Your honor is most welcome.

OTHELLO   Will you walk, sir?
O, Desdemona—   5

DESDEMONA   My lord?

OTHELLO   Get you to bed on th' instant; I will be returned
forthwith. Dismiss your attendant there.
Look't be done.

DESDEMONA   I will, my lord.   10
[Exit OTHELLO, with LODOVICO and Attendants]

EMILIA   How goes it now? He looks gentler than he did.

DESDEMONA   He says he will return incontinent.
He hath commanded me to go to bed,
And bade me to dismiss you.

EMILIA   Dismiss me?

DESDEMONA   It was his bidding; therefore, good Emilia,   15
Give me my nightly wearing, and adieu.
We must not now displease him.

EMILIA   I would you had never seen him!

DESDEMONA   So would I not. My love doth so approve him
That even his stubbornness, his checks, his frowns—   20
Prithee unpin me—have grace and favor in them.

EMILIA   I have laid those sheets you bade me on the bed.

DESDEMONA   All's one. Good faith, how foolish are our minds!
If I do die before thee, prithee shroud me
In one of those same sheets.   25

ACT IV, SCENE 3

Another room in Othello's castle in Cyprus.

[OTHELLO, LODOVICO, DESDEMONA, EMILIA, and company enter.]

LODOVICO	I urge you, sir, you don't have to escort me out.
OTHELLO	Please, I would enjoy the walk.
LODOVICO	Madam, good night. I thank you for your hospitality.
DESDEMONA	You are welcome, Lodovico.
OTHELLO	Shall we walk, Lodovico? Oh, Desdemona,
DESDEMONA	My lord?
OTHELLO	Go to bed immediately. I will come straight back. Dismiss Emilia for the night. Obey me.
DESDEMONA	I will, my lord. *[OTHELLO goes out with LODOVICO and company.]*
EMILIA	Is he better? He looks calmer than before.
DESDEMONA	He says he will come back immediately. He demanded that I go to bed and send you away.
EMILIA	Send me away?
DESDEMONA	That was his order. So, Emilia, hand me my nightgown and God go with you. We must do what he says.
EMILIA	I wish you had never met him!
DESDEMONA	I am not sorry. I love him so much that I find grace and joy even in his stubbornness, his willfulness, his frowns. Please unpin my hair.
EMILIA	I put your wedding sheets on the bed.
DESDEMONA	It isn't important. How trivial are our thoughts. If I should die before you, wrap me in a wedding sheet.

TRANSLATION

EMILIA	Come, come! You talk.
DESDEMONA	My mother had a maid called Barbary.
	She was in love; and he she loved proved mad
	And did forsake her. She had a song of 'Willow';
	An old thing 'twas; but it expressed her fortune,
	And she died singing it. That song to-night
	Will not go from my mind; I have much to do
	But to go hang my head all at one side
	And sing it like poor Barbary. Prithee dispatch.
EMILIA	Shall I go fetch your nightgown?
DESDEMONA	No, unpin me here.
	This Lodovico is a proper man.
EMILIA	A very handsome man.
DESDEMONA	He speaks well.
EMILIA	I know a lady in Venice would have walked
	barefoot to Palestine for a touch of his nether lip.
DESDEMONA	*[Sings]*
	'The poor soul sat sighing by a sycamore tree,
	Sing all a green willow;
	Her hand on her bosom, her head on her knee,
	Sing willow, willow, willow.
	The fresh streams ran by her and murmured her moans;
	Sing willow, willow, willow;
	Her salt tears fell from her, and soft'ned the stones'—
	Lay by these.
	'Sing willow, willow, willow'
	Prithee hie thee: he'll come anon.
	'Sing all a green willow must be my garland.
	Let nobody blame him; his scorn I approve'
	Nay, that's not next. Hark! who is't that knocks?
EMILIA	It is the wind.
DESDEMONA	*[Sings]*
	'I called my love false love; but what said he then?
	Sing willow, willow, willow:
	If I court moe women, you'll couch with moe men.'
	So, get thee gone; good night. Mine eyes do itch.
	Doth that bode weeping?

Line numbers in right margin: 30, 35, 40, 45, 50, 55

EMILIA	Please, don't talk about dying.
DESDEMONA	My mother had a lady-in-waiting named Barbary. She loved a man who abandoned her. She sang an old song called "Willow." The words described her bad luck; she died singing it. Tonight, I can't get that song out of my mind. I want to hang my head and sing "Willow" like poor Barbary. Please hurry.
EMILIA	Shall I bring your nightgown?
DESDEMONA	No. Unpin my hair. Lodovico seems like a gentleman.
EMILIA	He is also handsome.
DESDEMONA	He speaks well.
EMILIA	I know a woman in Venice who would have made a barefoot pilgrimage to the Holy Land for a touch of his bottom lip.
DESDEMONA	*[DESDEMONA sings.]* The poor woman mourned under a sycamore tree, singing of a green willow tree. She placed her hand on her heart and bowed her head to her knee, singing willow, willow, willow. The water flowed by and echoed her moan, singing willow, willow, willow. Salty tears flowed and softened the stones. Lay these over there. Sing willow, willow, willow. Hurry. He will be here soon. My crown must be made from a green willow limb. Don't blame him. I accept his scorn. No, that's not the next line. Listen, who is knocking?

ACT IV

EMILIA	It is the wind you hear.
DESDEMONA	*[DESDEMONA sings.]* "I called my love unfaithful, but what did he reply? Sing willow, willow, willow. If I woo more women, you will bed with more men." Go, good night. My eyes are itchy. Does that mean I will soon cry?

TRANSLATION

EMILIA	'Tis neither here nor there.

DESDEMONA I have heard it said so. O, these men, these men!
Dost thou in conscience think—tell me, Emilia—   60
That there be women do abuse their husbands
In such gross kind?

EMILIA	There be some such, no question.

DESDEMONA Wouldst thou do such a deed for all the world?

EMILIA Why, would not you?

DESDEMONA	No, by this heavenly light!

EMILIA Nor I neither by this heavenly light.   65
I might do't as well i' th' dark.

DESDEMONA Wouldst thou do such a deed for all the world?

EMILIA The world's a huge thing; it is a great
price for a small vice.

DESDEMONA Good troth, I think thou would'st not.   70

EMILIA By my troth, I think I should; and undo't when I
had done it. Marry, I would not do such a thing
for a joint-ring, nor for measures of lawn, nor for
gowns, petticoats, nor caps, nor any petty exhibition;
but, for all the whole world—'Ud's pity! who   75
would not make her husband a cuckold to make him
a monarch? I should venture purgatory for't.

DESDEMONA Beshrew me if I would do such a wrong
For the whole world.

EMILIA Why, the wrong is but a wrong i'th' world;   80
and having the world for your labor, 'tis a wrong in
your own world, and you might quickly make it right.

DESDEMONA I do not think there is any such woman.

EMILIA   It doesn't mean anything.

DESDEMONA   I have heard that interpretation of itchy eyes. Oh, men! Do you think, Emilia, that there are women who deceive their husbands by bedding with other men?

EMILIA   No question, there are unfaithful wives.

DESDEMONA   Would you be unfaithful to Iago?

EMILIA   Wouldn't you deceive Othello?

DESDEMONA   No, by the moon's light.

EMILIA   By the moon's light, neither would I betray Iago. But I might do it in the dark.

DESDEMONA   Would you commit adultery for all the world?

EMILIA   The world is a great reward for so small a sin.

DESDEMONA   Truly, I think you wouldn't do it.

EMILIA   I would and repent when I finished. I wouldn't do it for a finger ring, or a length of cotton cloth, or for dresses, slips, hats, or anything showy. But for the world, God's pity! Who would not make her husband a king by committing adultery. I would risk hell for it.

DESDEMONA   Forgive me if I would do wrong for the whole world.

EMILIA   Adultery is only a worldly sin. If you gained the whole world for committing a common sin, you could quickly correct it.

DESDEMONA   I don't think there is any woman who would do such a wrong.

ACT IV

TRANSLATION

Yes, a dozen; and as many to th' vantage as
would store the world they played for.   85
But I do think it is their husbands' faults
If wives do fall. Say that they slack their duties
And pour our treasures into foreign laps;
Or else break out in peevish jealousies,
Throwing restraint upon us; or say they strike us,   90
Or scant our former having in despite—
Why, we have galls; and though we have some grace,
Yet have we some revenge. Let husbands know
Their wives have sense like them. They see, and smell,
And have their palates both for sweet and sour,   95
As husbands have. What is it that they do
When they change us for others? Is it sport?
I think it is. And doth affection breed it?
I think it doth. Is't frailty that thus errs?
It is so too. And have not we affections,   100
Desires for sport, and frailty, as men have?
Then let them use us well; else let them know,
The ills we do, their ills instruct us so.

DESDEMONA   Good night, good night. God me such usage send,
Not to pick bad from bad, but by bad mend!   105
[Exeunt]

EMILIA   Yes, there's a dozen. And as many more would fill up the world they sinned for. I think husbands are at fault for their wives' sins. Men fail their domestic duties and spend their money on other women. Men nurture silly jealousies by keeping us under tight security. They threaten to hit us or spite us by withholding our house funds. Women respond with bad temper. We bestow forgiveness, but we also harbor vengeance. Husbands should know that wives feel the same emotions that they do. Women have vision, a sense of smell, and taste for sweet and sour foods, just like men. Why do they leave us for other women? Is it a game? I think it is. Does romance cause their disloyalty? I think it does. Is it human weakness that causes straying husbands? I think so. Don't women have the same tendency toward romance, games, and human weakness as men? Then let them treat us well. Let them understand that we learn our sins by observing their sins.

DESDEMONA   Good night, Emilia. God give me the choice not to pick from bad behaviors but to improve myself! *[DESDEMONA and EMILIA go out.]*

ACT IV

ACT V, SCENE 1

Cyprus. A street.

[Enter IAGO and RODERIGO]

| IAGO | Here, stand behind this bulk; straight will he come Wear thy good rapier bare, and put it home. Quick, quick! Fear nothing; I'll be at thy elbow. It makes us, or it mars us—think on that, And fix most firm thy resolution. | 5 |

| RODERIGO | Be near at hand; I may miscarry in't. | |

| IAGO | Here, at thy hand. Be bold, and take thy stand. *[Stands aside]* | |

| RODERIGO | I have no great devotion to the deed, And yet he hath given me satisfying reasons. 'Tis but a man gone. Forth my sword! He dies! | 10 |

| IAGO | I have rubbed this young quat almost to the sense, And he grows angry. Now whether he kill Cassio, Or Cassio him, or each do kill the other, Every way makes my gain. Live Roderigo, He calls me to a restitution large Of gold and jewels that I bobbed from him As gifts to Desdemona. It must not be. If Cassio do remain, He hath a daily beauty in his life That makes me ugly; and besides, the Moor May unfold me to him; there stand I in much peril. No, he must die. Be't so! I hear him coming. *[Enter CASSIO]* | 15 20 |

| RODERIGO | I know his gait. 'Tis he. Villain, thou diest! *[Makes a pass at CASSIO]* | |

| CASSIO | That thrust had been mine enemy indeed But that my coat is better than thou know'st. I will make proof of thine. *[Draws and wounds RODERIGO]* | 25 |

| RODERIGO | O, I am slain! *[IAGO darts from concealment behind CASSIO and wounds him in the leg. Exit]* | |

ACT V, SCENE 1

A street on the island of Cyprus.

[IAGO and RODERIGO enter.]

IAGO   Stand here behind this wall. Cassio will soon appear. Draw your two-edged sword and stab Cassio fatally. Be quick. Don't worry. I'll be behind you. Our success depends on your ambush. Keep our plan in mind and be steady.

RODERIGO   Stay close. I may fail.

IAGO   I'm here beside you. Be daring and face Cassio. *[IAGO stands apart from RODERIGO.]*

RODERIGO   I have no real urge to murder Cassio. But he has given me reasons to hate him. It is only one life lost. I strike with my sword! Cassio dies!

IAGO   I have rubbed this young pest to the nerve and made him mad. Whether Roderigo kills Cassio or Cassio kills Roderigo or both die in the attack, I am sure to win. If Roderigo lives, he will demand repayment of the gold and jewels I took from him to give to Desdemona. I can't let him live. If Cassio survives, he will continue outperforming me and making me look second rate. Also, Othello may tell Cassio of my lies about Cassio's seduction of Desdemona. If Cassio lives, I am in great danger. No, Cassio must die. On with the ambush! I hear him coming. *[CASSIO enters.]*

RODERIGO   I know Cassio's step. It is Cassio. Rogue, I will kill you! *[RODERIGO plunges his sword at CASSIO.]*

CASSIO   That thrust would have killed me, but my coat is thicker than you realized. I will thrust into your coat. *[CASSIO draws his sword and wounds RODERIGO.]*

RODERIGO   Oh, he has killed me! *[IAGO jumps from the wall behind CASSIO and wounds CASSIO in the leg. IAGO goes out.]*

ACT V

CASSIO	I am maimed for ever. Help, ho! Murder! murder! *[Exit]* *[Enter OTHELLO]*
OTHELLO	The voice of Cassio. Iago keeps his word.
RODERIGO	O, villain that I am!
OTHELLO	It is even so.
CASSIO	O, help, ho! light! a surgeon! 30
OTHELLO	'Tis he. O brave Iago, honest and just, That hast such noble sense of thy friend's wrong! Thou teachest me. Minion, your dear lies dead, And your unblest fate hies. Strumpet, I come. Forth of my heart those charms, thine eyes, are blotted. 35 Thy bed, lust-stained, shall with lust's blood be spotted. *[Exit]* *[Enter LODOVICO and GRATIANO]*
CASSIO	What, ho? No watch? No passage? Murder! murder!
GRATIANO	'Tis some mischance. The cry is very direful.
CASSIO	O, help!
LODOVICO	Hark! 40
RODERIGO	O wretched villain!
LODOVICO	Two or three groan. It is a heavy night. These may be counterfeits. Let's think't unsafe To come in to the cry without more help.
RODERIGO	Nobody come? Then shall I bleed to death. 45
LODOVICO	Hark! *[Enter IAGO with a light]*
GRATIANO	Here's one comes in his shirt, with light and weapons.
IAGO	Who's there? Whose noise is this that cries on murder?
LODOVICO	We do not know.
IAGO	Did not you hear a cry?
CASSIO	Here, here! For heaven's sake, help me! 50
IAGO	What's the matter?

CASSIO	I am seriously hurt. Help me! Murder! *[CASSIO goes out.]* *[OTHELLO enters.]*
OTHELLO	I hear Cassio calling. Iago kept his promise about killing Cassio.
RODERIGO	Oh, I am a criminal!
OTHELLO	Yes, you are.
CASSIO	Help! Bring a light! Call a surgeon!
OTHELLO	It's Cassio. Oh noble Iago, my honest friend, you have righted Cassio's wrong against me! You have set an example for me. Sweet Desdemona, your lover Cassio lies dead and you will die next. Whore, I am coming to kill you. I have blotted your charming eyes out of my heart. Your bed, marked with sin, I will spatter with your blood. *[OTHELLO goes out.]* *[LODOVICO and GRATIANO enter.]*
CASSIO	What—no security guard? No pedestrians? Murder!
GRATIANO	Sounds like a crime. His call is bloodcurdling.
CASSIO	Help me!
LODOVICO	Listen!
RODERIGO	Poor man!
LODOVICO	Two or three people are hurt. It is an overcast night. These calls may lure us into an ambush. We shouldn't answer the call without more people helping us.
RODERIGO	Is nobody coming? I am bleeding to death.
LODOVICO	Listen! *[IAGO enters with a light.]*
GRATIANO	Here comes a man in uniform carrying a light and swords.
IAGO	Who is there? Who calls out "murder"?
LODOVICO	We don't know.
IAGO	Did you hear a call for help?
CASSIO	Here I am! For God's sake, help me!
IAGO	What has happened?

ACT V

TRANSLATION

GRATIANO	This is Othello's ancient, as I take it.
LODOVICO	The same indeed, a very valiant fellow.
IAGO	What are you here that cry so grievously?
CASSIO	Iago? O, I am spoiled, undone by villains!
	Give me some help. 55
IAGO	O me, lieutenant! What villains have done this?
CASSIO	I think that one of them is hereabout
	And cannot make away.
IAGO	O treacherous villains!
	[To LODOVICO and GRATIANO]
	What are you there? Come in, and give some help.
RODERIGO	O, help me here! 60
CASSIO	That's one of them.
IAGO	O murd'rous slave! O villain!
	[Stabs RODERIGO]
RODERIGO	O damned Iago! O inhuman dog!
IAGO	Kill men i' th'dark?—Where be these bloody thieves?—
	How silent is this town!—Ho! murder! murder!
	What may you be? Are you of good or evil? 65
LODOVICO	As you shall prove us, praise us.
IAGO	Signior Lodovico?
LODOVICO	He, sir.
IAGO	I cry you mercy. Here's Cassio hurt by villains.
GRATIANO	Cassio? 70
IAGO	How is it, brother?
CASSIO	My leg is cut in two.
IAGO	Marry, heaven forbid!
	Light, gentlemen. I'll bind it with my shirt.
	[Enter BIANCA]
BIANCA	What is the matter, ho? Who is't that cried?
IAGO	Who is't that cried? 75

GRATIANO	This is Othello's flag bearer, I think.
LODOVICO	It is Iago, a brave man.
IAGO	Why do you cry so loud for help?
CASSIO	Iago? Oh, criminals have threatened my life! Help me.
IAGO	Oh, Lieutenant Cassio! Who attacked you?
CASSIO	I think one man lies nearby and can't escape.
IAGO	Oh, evil men! *[To LODOVICO and GRATIANO]* Who are you? Give me a hand.
RODERIGO	Oh, help me!
CASSIO	That's one of the attackers.
IAGO	You lowly sneak! You criminal! *[IAGO stabs RODERIGO.]*
RODERIGO	Damn you, Iago! You beast!
IAGO	Who would ambush men in the dark? Where are the attackers? This town is so silent! Murder! Murder! Who are you? Are you attackers or rescuers?
LODOVICO	We will prove ourselves to be good men.
IAGO	Lodovico?
LODOVICO	I am, sir.
IAGO	I need your help. Assassins have wounded Cassio.
GRATIANO	Cassio?
IAGO	How badly are you hurt?
CASSIO	My leg is sliced.
IAGO	God forbid! Hold up a light, gentlemen. I'll bind Cassio's leg with my shirt. *[BIANCA enters.]*
BIANCA	What is happening? Who is in danger?
IAGO	Who cried?

ACT V

TRANSLATION

BIANCA	O my dear Cassio! my sweet Cassio! O Cassio, Cassio, Cassio!
IAGO	O notable strumpet!—Cassio, may you suspect Who they should be that thus have mangled you?
CASSIO	No.
GRATIANO	I am sorry to find you thus. I have been to seek you.
IAGO	Lend me a garter. So. O for a chair To bear him easily hence!
BIANCA	Alas, he faints! O Cassio, Cassio, Cassio!
IAGO	Gentlemen all, I do suspect this trash To be a party in this injury.— Patience awhile, good Cassio.—Come, come! Lend me a light. Know we this face or no? Alas, my friend and my dear countryman Roderigo? No.—Yes, sure.—O heaven, Roderigo!
GRATIANO	What, of Venice?
IAGO	Even he, sir. Did you know him?
GRATIANO	Know him? Ay.
IAGO	Signior Gratiano? I cry you gentle pardon. These bloody accidents must excuse my manners That so neglected you.
GRATIANO	I am glad to see you.
IAGO	How do you, Cassio?—O, a chair, a chair!
GRATIANO	Roderigo?
IAGO	He, he, 'tis he! *[a chair brought in]* O, that's well said; the chair. Some good man bear him carefully from hence. I'll fetch the general's surgeon. *[To BIANCA]* For you, mistress, Save you your labor.—He that lies slain here, Cassio, Was my dear friend. What malice was between you?
CASSIO	None in the world; nor do I know the man.

80

85

90

95

100

BIANCA	Oh, my dear Cassio! my beloved Cassio! Oh, Cassio!
IAGO	I know this streetwalker! Cassio, do you suspect who stabbed your leg?
CASSIO	No.
GRATIANO	I regret seeing you hurt. I was on my way to find you.
IAGO	Does anyone have a garter? This will do. We need a stretcher to carry him without hurting him.
BIANCA	He has fainted! Oh, Cassio!
IAGO	Gentlemen, I suspect that this common woman took part in the ambush. Take it easy, Cassio. Hurry this way! Hand me a light. Does anyone know this man? No! Are you my friend Roderigo, a fellow Venetian? No. Yes, you are. Oh, God, Roderigo!
GRATIANO	Roderigo of Venice?
IAGO	It is Roderigo. Did you know him?
GRATIANO	Yes, I knew him.
IAGO	Gratiano, pardon me. These attacks made me forget my manners.
GRATIANO	I am pleased to see you.
IAGO	How are you, Cassio? Bring a stretcher!
GRATIANO	Is it Roderigo?
IAGO	It is Roderigo! *[Someone brings in a stretcher.]* Oh, good, a stretcher at last. Some good person help carry him carefully away. I'll get General Othello's surgeon. *[To BIANCA]* Don't bother, ma'am, to offer first aid. Cassio, this dead man was my close friend Roderigo. What was your quarrel with him?
CASSIO	I had no quarrel with Roderigo. I didn't know him.

ACT V

TRANSLATION

IAGO	*[To BIANCA]* What, look you pale—O, bear him out o' th' air.
	[CASSIO and RODERIGO are borne off]
	Stay you, good gentlemen.—Look you pale, mistress?— 105
	Do you perceive the gastness of her eye?—
	Nay, if you stare, we shall hear more anon.
	Behold her well; I pray you look upon her.
	Do you see, gentlemen? Nay, guiltiness will speak,
	Though tongues were out of use. 110
	[Enter EMILIA]
EMILIA	'Las, what's the matter? What's the matter husband?
IAGO	Cassio hath here been set on in the dark
	By Roderigo, and fellows that are scaped.
	He's almost slain, and Roderigo dead.
EMILIA	Alas, good gentlemen! alas, good Cassio! 115
IAGO	This is the fruit of whoring. Prithee, Emilia,
	Go know of Cassio where he supped to-night.
	[To BIANCA] What, do you shake at that?
BIANCA	He supped at my house; but I therefore shake not.
IAGO	O, did he so? I charge you go with me. 120
EMILIA	Fie, fie upon thee, strumpet!
BIANCA	I am no strumpet, but of life as honest
	As you that thus abuse me.
EMILIA	As I? Foh! fie upon thee!
IAGO	Kind gentlemen, let's go see poor Cassio dressed.
	[To BIANCA] Come, mistress, you must tell's another tale. 125
	Emilia, run you to the citadel
	And tell my lord and lady what hath happed.
	[Exit EMILIA]
	Will you go on afore? *[Exeunt all but IAGO]*
	This is the night
	That either makes me or fordoes me quite. *[Exit]*

IAGO	*[To BIANCA]* You look pale, Bianca. Carry Cassio to a sheltered place. *[Onlookers carry CASSIO and RODERIGO away.]* Please wait, Lodovico and Gratiano. Bianca, are you faint? Do you gentlemen see the terror in her eyes? If you are frightened, you can tell us later what you know about this ambush. Take care of her. Look out for her. Do you notice, Lodovico and Gratiano? You can see signs of guilt, even though the guilty party says nothing. *[EMILIA enters.]*
EMILIA	Alas, what has happened? What happened here, Iago?
IAGO	Roderigo and some runaways ambushed Cassio in the dark. Roderigo is dying. Cassio is gravely hurt.
EMILIA	Oh, worthy gentlemen! Cassio is a good man.
IAGO	It is Cassio's fault for patronizing a prostitute. Emilia, find out where Cassio ate dinner tonight. *[To BIANCA]* Does that question make you tremble?
BIANCA	He ate dinner with me, but I am not trembling.
IAGO	Oh, did he? I demand that you accompany me.
EMILIA	Shame on you, streetwalker!
BIANCA	I am not a whore. I am as decent a person as you.
EMILIA	You compare yourself to me? Shame on you!
IAGO	Gentlemen, let us be certain that the surgeon is treating Cassio's wound. *[To BIANCA]* Come, ma'am, you must tell more of your whereabouts tonight. Emilia, hurry to the fort and report to Othello and Desdemona Roderigo's death and Cassio's wound. *[EMILIA goes out.]* Will you lead the way, Lodovico and Gratiano? *[Everyone departs but IAGO.]* Tonight, either my plan succeeds or I am ruined. *[IAGO goes out.]*

ACT V

TRANSLATION

ACT V, SCENE 2

A bedchamber in the castle.

[DESDEMONA asleep in her bed; Enter OTHELLO with a light]

OTHELLO	It is the cause, it is the cause, my soul.
	Let me not name it to you, you chaste stars!
	It is the cause. Yet I'll not shed her blood,
	Nor scar that whiter skin of hers than snow,
	And smooth as monumental alabaster.

It is the cause, it is the cause, my soul.
Let me not name it to you, you chaste stars!
It is the cause. Yet I'll not shed her blood,
Nor scar that whiter skin of hers than snow,
And smooth as monumental alabaster.   5
Yet she must die, else she'll betray more men.
Put out the light, and then put out the light.
If I quench thee, thou flaming minister,
I can again thy former light restore,
Should I repent me; but once put out thy light,   10
Thou cunning'st pattern of excelling nature,
I know not where is that Promethean heat
That can thy light relume. When I have plucked the rose,
I cannot give it vital growth again;
It needs must wither, I'll smell thee on the tree.   15
[He kisses her]
O balmy breath, that dost almost persuade
Justice to break her sword! One more, one more!
Be thus when thou art dead, and I will kill thee,
And love thee after. One more, and this the last!
So sweet was ne'er so fatal. I must weep,   20
But they are cruel tears. This sorrow's heavenly;
It strikes where it doth love. She wakes.

DESDEMONA   Who's there? Othello?

OTHELLO   Ay, Desdemona.

DESDEMONA   Will you come to bed, my lord?

OTHELLO   Have you prayed to-night, Desdemon?   25

DESDEMONA   Ay, my lord.

OTHELLO   If you bethink yourself of any crime
Unreconciled as yet to heaven and grace,
Solicit for it straight.

ACT V, SCENE 2

A bedroom in the castle on Cyprus.

[While DESDEMONA sleeps on the bed, OTHELLO enters the room with a light.]

OTHELLO   There is just cause for suspicion, my soul. I won't say the vulgar word to you, pure stars! There is just cause. I can't shed her blood or mar her creamy white skin. I must kill her before she seduces more men. Put out the candle, and then kill her. If I put out the candle and change my mind, I can relight it. But when I kill you, wondrous work of nature, no heat can revive your life. When I pick the rose, I can't reattach it to the branch. The rose will wither. I must smell its fragrance while it's attached to the branch. *[OTHELLO kisses DESDEMONA.]* Oh, sweet breath, you almost convince me to forget vengeance. One more kiss! one more! Stay beautiful in death. I will kill you and continue admiring your loveliness. One more kiss, the last one! Nothing so dear was ever so danger-ous. I can't stop crying, but my tears are cruel. My grief is like God's grief. He strikes the people whom he loves. Desdemona is stirring.

DESDEMONA   Othello? Is that you?

OTHELLO   Yes, Desdemona.

DESDEMONA   Are you coming to bed, my lord?

OTHELLO   Did you say your prayers, Desdemona?

DESDEMONA   Yes, my lord.

OTHELLO   If you hide any sin from God, ask immediately for pardon.

DESDEMONA	Alack, my lord, what may you mean by that?
OTHELLO	Well, do it, and be brief; I will walk by. 30 I would not kill thy unprepared spirit. No, heaven forfend! I would not kill thy soul.
DESDEMONA	Talk you of killing?
OTHELLO	Ay, I do.
DESDEMONA	Then heaven Have mercy on me!
OTHELLO	Amen, with all my heart!
DESDEMONA	If you say so, I hope you will not kill me. 35
OTHELLO	Hum!
DESDEMONA	And yet I fear you; for you are fatal then When your eyes roll so. Why I should fear I know not, Since guiltiness I know not; but yet I feel I fear.
OTHELLO	Think on thy sins. 40
DESDEMONA	They are loves I bear to you.
OTHELLO	Ay, and for that thou diest.
DESDEMONA	That death's unnatural that kills for loving. Alas, why gnaw you so your nether lip? Some bloody passion shakes your very frame. These are portents; but yet I hope, I hope, 45 They do not point on me.
OTHELLO	Peace and be still!
DESDEMONA	I will so. What's the matter?
OTHELLO	That handkerchief which I so loved and gave thee Thou gav'st to Cassio.
DESDEMONA	No, by my life and soul! Send for the man and ask him. 50
OTHELLO	Sweet soul, take heed, Take heed of perjury; thou art on thy deathbed.
DESDEMONA	Ay, but not yet to die.

ORIGINAL

DESDEMONA	Oh, dear, my lord, what do you mean by asking for forgiveness?
OTHELLO	Confess your sins quickly. I will leave you in privacy. I wouldn't murder you with sins on your soul. No, God forbid! I would not jeopardize your soul.
DESDEMONA	Do you speak of killing me?
OTHELLO	Yes, I do.
DESDEMONA	God be merciful to me!
OTHELLO	Yes, I heartily agree.
DESDEMONA	I hope you don't intend murder, if you believe in mercy.
OTHELLO	Hmm.
DESDEMONA	I am afraid of you. You are dangerous when you roll your eyes. I have no guilty reason to fear punishment, but I am afraid.
OTHELLO	Think over your sins.
DESDEMONA	My sin is love for you.
OTHELLO	Yes, and for sinning against me, you must die.
DESDEMONA	It makes no sense to kill me because you love me. Why do you chew your bottom lip? Some fierce emotion makes you tremble. This behavior suggests a frightful fate. I hope you mean me no harm.
OTHELLO	Quiet. Be still!
DESDEMONA	I will be silent. What is troubling you?
OTHELLO	The precious handkerchief that I gave you, you gave to Cassio.
DESDEMONA	No, I didn't, I swear on my life and soul! Send for Cassio and ask him.
OTHELLO	Dear Desdemona, be careful of lying. You are about to die.
DESDEMONA	I should not die yet.

TRANSLATION

OTHELLO	Yes, presently.
	Therefore confess thee freely of thy sin;
	For to deny each article with oath
	Cannot remove nor choke the strong conception 55
	That I do groan withal. Thou art to die.
DESDEMONA	Then Lord have mercy on me!
OTHELLO	I say amen.
DESDEMONA	And have you mercy too! I never did
	Offend you in my life; never loved Cassio
	But with such general warranty of heaven 60
	As I might love. I never gave him token.
OTHELLO	By heaven, I saw my handkerchief in's hand!
	O perjured woman! thou dost stone my heart,
	And mak'st me call what I intend to do
	A murder, which I thought a sacrifice. 65
	I saw the handkerchief.
DESDEMONA	He found it then.
	I never gave it him. Send for him hither.
	Let him confess a truth.
OTHELLO	He hath confessed.
DESDEMONA	What, my lord?
OTHELLO	That he hath used thee. 70
DESDEMONA	How? unlawfully?
OTHELLO	Ay.
DESDEMONA	He will not say so.
OTHELLO	No, his mouth is stopped.
	Honest Iago hath ta'en order for't.
DESDEMONA	O, my fear interprets. What, is he dead?
OTHELLO	Had all his hairs been lives, my great revenge
	Had stomach for them all. 75
DESDEMONA	Alas, he is betrayed, and I undone!
OTHELLO	Out, strumpet! Weep'st thou for him to my face?
DESDEMONA	O, banish me, my lord, but kill me not!

OTHELLO	Yes, soon. Confess your faults completely. Your denials don't remove my suspicions, which make me groan. You are going to die.
DESDEMONA	God pity me!
OTHELLO	I hope God does pity you.
DESDEMONA	And may you pity me! I have committed no wrong against you. I loved Cassio only as a friend. I gave him no love token.
OTHELLO	By God, I saw him carrying my handkerchief! Oh, lying woman! You turn my heart to stone. I meant to sacrifice you to justice, but I must murder you. I saw the handkerchief.
DESDEMONA	Cassio must have found it. I didn't give Cassio the handkerchief. Send for Cassio and hear his side of the story.
OTHELLO	He confessed his wrong.
DESDEMONA	What, sir?
OTHELLO	He confessed that he was your lover.
DESDEMONA	His lover?
OTHELLO	Yes.
DESDEMONA	He will not say such a thing.
OTHELLO	No, he will never speak again. Iago silenced Cassio forever.
DESDEMONA	I'm afraid to ask. Is Cassio dead?
OTHELLO	If he had as many lives as he had hairs, I would have killed him that many times.
DESDEMONA	Someone betrayed him. I have no hope!
OTHELLO	Stop, whore! Would you weep for Cassio in front of me?
DESDEMONA	Exile me, Othello. Don't kill me!

ACT V

TRANSLATION

OTHELLO	Down, strumpet!	
DESDEMONA	Kill me to-morrow; let me live to-night!	80
OTHELLO	Nay, an you strive—	
DESDEMONA	But half an hour!	
OTHELLO	Being done, there is no pause.	
DESDEMONA	But while I say one prayer!	
OTHELLO	It is too late. *[Smothers her]*	
DESDEMONA	O Lord, Lord, Lord! *[EMILIA at the door]*	
EMILIA	*[Calls within]* My lord, my lord! What, ho, my lord, my lord!	85
OTHELLO	What noise is this? Not dead? not yet quite dead? I that am cruel am yet merciful; I would not have thee linger in thy pain. So, so.	
EMILIA	*[Within]* What, ho! my lord, my lord!	
OTHELLO	Who's there?	
EMILIA	*[Within]* O, good my lord, I would speak a word with you!	90
OTHELLO	Yes, 'tis Emilia.—By and by.—She's dead.— 'Tis like she comes to speak of Cassio's death. The noise was here. Ha! no more moving? Still as the grave.—Shall she come in? Were't good? I think she stirs again. No.—What's best to do? If she come in, she'll sure speak to my wife. My wife! my wife! what wife? I have no wife. O, insupportable! O heavy hour! Methinks it should be now a huge eclipse Of sun and moon, and that th' affrighted globe Should yawn at alteration.	95 100
EMILIA	*[Within]* I do beseech you That I may speak with you, O good my lord!	

OTHELLO	Lie down, whore!
DESDEMONA	Murder me tomorrow. Let me live tonight!
OTHELLO	No, even if you struggle.
DESDEMONA	Let me live another half hour.
OTHELLO	I have made up my mind. There can be no delay.
DESDEMONA	Let me pray before I die!
OTHELLO	It is too late for you. *[OTHELLO suffocates DESDEMONA.]*
DESDEMONA	Oh, lord! *[EMILIA comes to the bedroom door.]*
EMILIA	*[EMILIA calls through the door.]* My lord! What is happening, Othello!
OTHELLO	Who is calling? Desdemona is still alive. She lingers. Even though I am cruel, I would kill her painlessly. I would not leave you suffering. So, I have finished.
EMILIA	*[From outside the door]* What is happening? My lord!
OTHELLO	Who is calling?
EMILIA	*[From outside the door]* Othello, please speak to me!
OTHELLO	Yes, it is Emilia. Soon. Desdemona's dead. I assume Emilia has come to report Cassio's murder. I heard a noise. You are motionless? Desdemona is as still as a corpse. Shall I let Emilia in? Is that a good idea? I think Desdemona is still breathing. No. What should I do? If Emilia comes in, she will speak to Desdemona. To my wife? What wife? I am wifeless. Oh, unforgivable deed! A grievous time! The sun and moon should go dark. The earth should gasp in fear of so great a loss.
EMILIA	*[Outside the door]* Please, Othello, I must speak to you.

ACT V

TRANSLATION

OTHELLO	I had forgot thee. O, come in, Emilia.
	Soft, by and by.—Let me the curtains draw.— 105
	[Closes the bed-curtains]
	Where art thou? *[Opens the door]*
	[Enter EMILIA]
	What's the matter with thee now?

EMILIA   O my good lord, yonder's foul murder done!

OTHELLO   What? Now?

EMILIA   But now, my lord.

OTHELLO   It is the very error of the moon.   110
                She comes more nearer earth than she was wont
                And makes men mad.

EMILIA   Cassio, my lord, hath killed a young Venetian.
                Called Roderigo.

OTHELLO   Roderigo killed?
                And Cassio killed?   115

EMILIA   No, Cassio is not killed.

OTHELLO   Not Cassio killed? Then murder's out of tune,
                And sweet revenge grows harsh.

DESDEMONA   O, falsely, falsely murdered!

EMILIA   O Lord! what cry is that?

OTHELLO   That? What?

EMILIA   Out and alas! that was my lady's voice.   120
                Help! help, ho! help! O lady, speak again!
                Sweet Desdemona! O sweet mistress, speak!

DESDEMONA   A guiltless death I die.

EMILIA   O, who hath done this deed?

DESDEMONA   Nobody—I myself. Farewell.   125
                Commend me to my kind lord. O, farewell!
                [She dies]

OTHELLO   Why, how should she be murd'red?

EMILIA   Alas, who knows?

OTHELLO   You heard her say herself, it was not I.

EMILIA   She said so. I must needs report the truth.

ORIGINAL

OTHELLO	I had forgotten that you were knocking. Come in, Emilia. Be quiet, please. Let me pull the bed drapes. *[OTHELLO shuts the bed drapes.]* Where are you? *[OTHELLO opens the door.]* *[EMILIA enters the bedroom.]* What do you want at this hour?
EMILIA	My lord, someone has committed murder!
OTHELLO	At this hour?
EMILIA	Just now, Othello.
OTHELLO	The moon causes wrongs. When the moon approaches earth, she drives people insane.
EMILIA	Cassio has murdered Roderigo, a young Venetian.
OTHELLO	Roderigo is dead? And Cassio has died?
EMILIA	No, Cassio survived.
OTHELLO	Cassio is still alive? The wrong man is dead. Revenge has turned evil.
DESDEMONA	Oh, I am wrongly killed.
EMILIA	Oh, Othello! Who said that?
OTHELLO	Said what?
EMILIA	No! That was Desdemona's voice. Help! Oh, Desdemona, speak again! My sweet lady! Desdemona, speak up!
DESDEMONA	I am dying innocent of wrong.
EMILIA	Oh, who has killed Desdemona?
DESDEMONA	No one. It is my fault. Goodbye. Say farewell to Othello for me. Goodbye! *[DESDEMONA dies.]*
OTHELLO	Why would anyone murder her?
EMILIA	I don't know.
OTHELLO	You heard her say that I did not attack her.
EMILIA	That is what she said. I must report what I heard.

ACT V

TRANSLATION

| OTHELLO | She's like a liar gone to burning hell! | 130 |
| | 'Twas I that killed her. | |

| EMILIA | O, the more angel she, |
| | And you the blacker devil! |

| OTHELLO | She turned to folly, and she was a whore. |

| EMILIA | Thou dost belie her, and thou art a devil. |

| OTHELLO | She was false as water. | 135 |

| EMILIA | Thou art rash as fire to say |
| | That she was false. O, she was heavenly true! |

OTHELLO	Cassio did top her. Ask thy husband else.	
	O, I were damned beneath all depth in hell	
	But that I did proceed upon just grounds	
	To this extremity. Thy husband knew it all.	140

| EMILIA | My husband? |

| OTHELLO | Thy husband. |

| EMILIA | That she was false to wedlock? |

OTHELLO	Ay, with Cassio. Nay, had she been true,	
	If heaven would make me such another world	145
	Of one entire and perfect chrysolite,	
	I'ld not have sold her for it.	

| EMILIA | My husband? |

OTHELLO	Ay, 'twas he that told me first.	
	An honest man he is, and hates the slime	
	That sticks on filthy deeds.	150

| EMILIA | My husband? |

| OTHELLO | What needs this iterance? Woman, I say thy husband. |

| EMILIA | O mistress, villainy hath made mocks with love! |
| | My husband say that she was false? |

OTHELLO	He, woman.	
	I say, thy husband. Dost understand the word?	
	My friend, thy husband; honest, honest Iago.	155

EMILIA	If he say so, may his pernicious soul
	Rot half a grain a day! he lies to th' heart.
	She was too fond of her most filthy bargain.

OTHELLO	She is lying. I killed her.
EMILIA	You are a black demon for killing so sweet an angel!
OTHELLO	She became a seducer; she was a slut.
EMILIA	You are lying. You are the evil one.
OTHELLO	She was as untamable as flowing water.
EMILIA	You are wrong to lie about her. She was godly and honest!
OTHELLO	Cassio had sex with her. Iago is a witness. I would be damned indeed if I killed Desdemona without reason. Iago was the witness.
EMILIA	My husband?
OTHELLO	Your husband.
EMILIA	He claimed that Desdemona was an impure wife?
OTHELLO	Yes, with Cassio. If she had been faithful and God had offered me a perfect globe of topaz, I would not have given her up for it.
EMILIA	My husband?
OTHELLO	Yes, Iago first told me of her affair with Cassio. Iago is honest and devoted to clean living.
EMILIA	My husband?
OTHELLO	Why do you keep asking? Emilia, I learned it from Iago.
EMILIA	Oh, Desdemona, a criminal has toyed with your love! My husband charged her with impurity?
OTHELLO	Yes, Emilia. It was Iago. Don't you understand? Iago, my friend, your husband, an honest man.
EMILIA	If he said Desdemona was unfaithful, may Iago's soul rot a tiny bit each day! He is false to the core. She was innocent of a corrupt bargain.

ACT V

OTHELLO	Ha!
EMILIA	Do thy worst.
	This deed of thine is no more worthy heaven 160
	Than thou wast worthy her.
OTHELLO	Peace, you were best.
EMILIA	Thou hast not half the power to do me harm
	As I have to be hurt. O gull! O dolt!
	As ignorant as dirt! thou hast done a deed—
	I care not for thy sword; I'll make thee known, 165
	Though I lost twenty lives. Help! help! O, help!
	The Moor hath killed my mistress! Murder! murder!
	[Enter MONTANO, GRATIANO, IAGO, and others]
MONTANO	What is the matter? How now, general?
EMILIA	O, are you come, Iago? You have done well,
	That men must lay their murders on your neck. 170
GRATIANO	What is the matter?
EMILIA	Disprove this villain, if thou be'st a man.
	He says thou told'st him that his wife was false.
	I know thou did'st not; thou'rt not such a villain.
	Speak, for my heart is full. 175
IAGO	I told him what I thought, and told no more
	Than what he found himself was apt and true.
EMILIA	But did you ever tell him she was false?
IAGO	I did.
EMILIA	You told a lie, an odious damned lie! 180
	Upon my soul, a lie! a wicked lie!
	She false with Cassio? Did you say with Cassio?
IAGO	With Cassio, mistress. Go to, charm your tongue.
EMILIA	I will not charm my tongue; I am bound to speak:
	My mistress here lies murdered in her bed— 185
ALL	O heavens forfend!
EMILIA	And your reports have set the murder on.
OTHELLO	Nay, stare not, masters. It is true indeed.
GRATIANO	'Tis a strange truth.

OTHELLO	Ha!
EMILIA	Do whatever you want! Your vengeance is no more worthy of blessing than you were worthy of her as a wife.
OTHELLO	You had better shut up.
EMILIA	You have half the capability of hurting me than I have of hurting myself. Oh, fool! You idiot! You are stupid as dirt! You have done something—I'm not afraid of your weapon. I'll tell the world, if you killed me twenty times. Help, help! Othello has killed Desdemona. Murder, murder! *[MONTANO, GRATIANO, IAGO, and others enter the bedroom.]*
MONTANO	What is wrong? What have you done, General Othello?
EMILIA	I am glad you are here, Iago. You have committed evil that Othello charges against you.
GRATIANO	What has happened?
EMILIA	Correct Othello, if you are a man. He claims that you told him Desdemona was unfaithful. You couldn't be so vile a rogue as to have said that. Tell him, for I am angry.
IAGO	I told him what I thought and no more than he discovered with his own eyes.
EMILIA	Did you tell him that Desdemona was a seducer?
IAGO	I did.
EMILIA	You told Othello a lie, a hateful, damnable lie! I pledge my soul that you told an evil lie! Did you claim that she had an affair with Cassio?
IAGO	She was Cassio's lover, Emilia. Hush. Hold your tongue.
EMILIA	I will not hold my tongue. I must speak. Othello has strangled Desdemona in her bed.
ALL	God forbid!
EMILIA	Your lies have caused the murder.
OTHELLO	Don't gape at me, sirs. I did kill her.
GRATIANO	You are oddly eager to confess.

ACT V

MONTANO	O monstrous act!	190

EMILIA
　　　　　　　　　　Villainy, villainy, villainy!
I think upon't—I think I smell't!—O villainy!
I thought so then.—I'll kill myself for grief.—
O villainy, villainy!

IAGO　　What, are you mad? I charge you get you home.

EMILIA　　Good gentlemen, let me have leave to speak.　195
'Tis proper I obey him, but not now.
Perchance, Iago, I will ne'er go home.

OTHELLO　　O! O! O! *[Falls on the bed]*

EMILIA
　　　　　　　　　　　　Nay, lay thee down and roar!
For thou hast killed the sweetest innocent
That e'er did lift up eye.　200

OTHELLO
　　　　　　　　　　　O, she was foul! *[Rises]*
I scarce did know you, uncle. There lies your niece,
Whose breath, indeed, these hands have newly stopped.
I know this act shows horrible and grim.

GRATIANO　　Poor Desdemon! I am glad thy father's dead.
Thy match was mortal to him, and pure grief　205
Shore his old thread in twain. Did he live now,
This sight would make him do a desperate turn;
Yea, curse his better angel from his side,
And fall to reprobation.

OTHELLO　　'Tis pitiful; but yet Iago knows　210
That she with Cassio hath the act of shame
A thousand times committed. Cassio confessed it;
And she did gratify his amorous works
With that recognizance and pledge of love
Which I first gave her. I saw it in his hand.　215
It was a handkerchief, an antique token
My father gave my mother.

EMILIA　　O God! O heavenly God!

IAGO　　Zounds, hold your peace!

EMILIA
　　　　　　　　　　'Twill out, 'twill out! I peace?
No, I will speak as liberal as the north.　220
Let heaven and men and devils, let them all,
All, all, cry shame against me, yet I'll speak.

ORIGINAL

MONTANO	What a monstrous deed!
EMILIA	Crime! I see it in my mind. I smell crime. Oh, evil! I suspected wrong when you questioned her earlier. Grief will kill me. Oh, evil deed!
IAGO	Why are you raving? I demand that you go home now.
EMILIA	Gentlemen, listen to what I have to say. I must obey as a wife should, but not until this matter is settled. Maybe I can never go home to you again, Iago.
OTHELLO	Oh! oh! oh! [OTHELLO collapses on the bed.]
EMILIA	Indeed, you should lie there and scream! You have murdered the sweetest girl who ever lived.
OTHELLO	She was corrupt! [OTHELLO rises from the bed.] I don't know you well, Uncle Gratiano. There lies Desdemona, your niece, whom I have just strangled. My deed looks cruel and terrible.
GRATIANO	Poor Desdemona! I am glad Brabantio died before this time. Your elopement killed him. He died of grief. If he were still alive, your corpse would drive him to desperate measures. He would curse his guardian angel and sink into damnable sin.
OTHELLO	It is woeful that she is dead. Iago is witness to Cassio's adultery with Desdemona a thousand times. Cassio confessed his wrong. She repaid his sexual attentions with the first gift that I gave her. I saw it in Cassio's hand. It was the handkerchief that my father gave my mother.
EMILIA	Oh, God! Oh, God in heaven!
IAGO	God's wounds, be quiet!
EMILIA	I must tell the truth! You want me silent? No, I will speak words as loosely as the north wind blows. Let God and people and demons all speak and shame me, but I will tell the truth.

ACT V

TRANSLATION

IAGO	Be wise, and get you home.
EMILIA	I will not.
	[IAGO draws and threatens EMILIA]
GRATIANO	Fie!
	Your sword upon a woman?
EMILIA	O thou dull Moor, that handkerchief thou speak'st of 225
	I found by fortune, and did give my husband;
	For often with a solemn earnestness—
	More than indeed belonged to such a trifle—
	He begged of me to steal't.
IAGO	Villainous whore!
EMILIA	She give it Cassio? No, alas, I found it, 230
	And I did give't my husband.
IAGO	Filth, thou liest!
EMILIA	By heaven, I do not, I do not, gentlemen.
	O murd'rous coxcomb! what should such a fool
	Do with so good a wife?
OTHELLO	Are there no stones in heaven
	But what serves for the thunder? Precious villain! 235
	[THE MOOR runs at IAGO but is disarmed by MONTANO. IAGO kills his wife]
GRATIANO	The woman falls. Sure he hath killed his wife.
EMILIA	Ay, ay. O, lay me by my mistress' side. *[Exit IAGO]*
GRATIANO	He's gone, but his wife's killed.
MONTANO	'Tis a notorious villain. Take you this weapon,
	Which I have here recovered from the Moor. 240
	Come, guard the door without. Let him not pass,
	But kill him rather. I'll after that same villain,
	For 'tis a damned slave.
	[Exit MONTANO, with all but OTHELLO and EMILIA]
OTHELLO	I am not valiant neither;
	But every puny whipster gets my sword.
	But why should honor outlive honesty? 245
	Let it go all.

IAGO	Do as I say and go home.
EMILIA	I will not. *[IAGO draws his sword and threatens to stab EMILIA.]*
GRATIANO	Shame! You draw a sword against a woman?
EMILIA	Oh, you stupid Moor, the handkerchief you mention I found and gave to Iago. Often and seriously, Iago begged me to steal it.
IAGO	Lying prostitute!
EMILIA	You think Desdemona gave it to Cassio? You're wrong. I found it. I passed it on to Iago.
IAGO	Corrupt, lying wife!
EMILIA	By God, gentlemen, I tell the truth. Oh, evil trickster! Why would a fool like Othello deserve a wife as good as Desdemona?
OTHELLO	Is there no noisemaker in heaven except those that make thunder? Dire felon! *[OTHELLO thrusts his sword at IAGO; MONTANO takes the sword. IAGO kills EMILIA.]*
GRATIANO	Emilia collapsed. Iago has murdered his wife.
EMILIA	Please, lay my body by Desdemona's corpse. *[IAGO goes out.]*
GRATIANO	Iago has fled after murdering Emilia.
MONTANO	Iago is an unspeakable felon. Seize this sword. Post a guard at the door. Kill Othello if he tries to escape. I will apprehend Iago, who is a damnable villain. *[MONTANO and the others go out, leaving OTHELLO and EMILIA in the bedroom with DESDEMONA's corpse.]*
OTHELLO	I am unworthy. But every scrawny upstart I strike with my weapon. Why should my reputation outlive my honesty? Let it all go.

ACT V

TRANSLATION

EMILIA	What did thy song bode, lady?

EMILIA   What did thy song bode, lady?
Hark, canst thou hear me? I will play the swan,
And die in music. *[Sings]* 'Willow, willow, willow.'
Moor, she was chaste. She loved thee, cruel Moor:
So come my soul to bliss as I speak true.   250
So speaking as I think, I die, I die. *[She dies]*

OTHELLO   I have another weapon in this chamber;
It is a sword of Spain, the ice-brook's temper.
O, here it is.—Uncle, I must come forth.

GRATIANO   *[Within]* If thou attempt it, it will cost thee dear.   255
Thou hast no weapon, and perforce must suffer.

OTHELLO   Look in upon me then and speak with me,
Or, naked as I am, I will assault thee.
[Enter GRATIANO]

GRATIANO   What is the matter?

OTHELLO   Behold, I have a weapon;
A better never did itself sustain   260
Upon a soldier's thigh. I have seen the day
That with this little arm and this good sword
I have made my way through more impediments
Than twenty times your stop. But O vain boast!
Who can control his fate? 'Tis not so now.   265
Be not afraid, though you do see me weaponed.
Here is my journey's end, here is my butt,
And very seamark of my utmost sail.
Do you go back dismayed? 'Tis a lost fear.
Man but a rush against Othello's breast,   270
And he retires. Where should Othello go?
Now, how dost thou look now? O ill-starred wench!
Pale as thy smock! When we shall meet at compt,
This look of thine will hurl my soul from heaven,
And fiends will snatch at it. Cold, cold, my girl?   275
Even like thy chastity.
O cursed, cursed slave! Whip me, ye devils,
From the possession of this heavenly sight!
Blow me about in winds! roast me in sulphur!
Wash me in steep-down gulfs of liquid fire!   280
O Desdemona, Desdemona! dead!
O! O! O!
*[Enter LODOVICO, MONTANO, IAGO as prisoner, and Officers;
CASSIO in a chair]*

EMILIA	What did you mean by your song, Desdemona? Can you hear me? I will be a swan and die singing my one note. *[EMILIA sings.]* "Willow, willow, willow." Othello, she was pure. She loved you, cruel man. May I go to heaven if I tell the truth. I die with these words. *[EMILIA dies.]*
OTHELLO	I have another weapon in this room. It is a Spanish sword that was heated in the forge, then cooled in an icy stream. I've found it. Uncle, I must exit this room.
GRATIANO	*[From the other side of the door]* If you try to leave, you risk your life. Without a weapon, you would lose the fight.
OTHELLO	Come talk to me. Else, unarmed, I will attack you. *[GRATIANO enters the bedroom.]*
GRATIANO	What do you want?
OTHELLO	See, I am armed. This is the best that a soldier can carry. In past days, I have slashed my way with this sword through twenty guards. What empty bragging! Who can control destiny? I can't. Don't worry, even though I am armed. This is the end of my life, my limit, the aim of my journey. Are you surprised? It is an unnecessary fear. Strike Othello's chest with a weed and he withdraws. Where should I go? How do you appear to me now, Desdemona? Unfortunate girl! You are as pale as your nightgown! When we meet on judgment day, your inno-cent expression will damn my soul. Demons will seize me. Are you already cold, my girl? You were pure. Oh, I am a doomed, doomed drudge! Lash me, you demons, for looking on this angelic woman! Toss me in gales! Cook me in sulfur! Wash me in sloping bays of liquid flame! Oh, Desdemona, Desdemona, she's dead! Oh, oh, oh. *[LODOVICO, MONTANO, and officers enter the bedroom with IAGO in custody and CASSIO on a stretcher.]*

ACT V

TRANSLATION

LODOVICO	Where is this rash and most unfortunate man?	
OTHELLO	That's he that was Othello. Here I am.	
LODOVICO	Where is that viper? Bring the villain forth.	285

OTHELLO
I look down towards his feet—but that's a fable.
If that thou be'st a devil, I cannot kill thee.
[Wounds IAGO]

LODOVICO
Wrench his sword from him.
[OTHELLO is disarmed]

IAGO   I bleed, sir, but not killed.

OTHELLO
I am not sorry neither. I'ld have thee live;
For in my sense, 'tis happiness to die.   290

LODOVICO
O thou Othello that wert once so good,
Fall'n in the practice of a damned slave,
What shall be said to thee?

OTHELLO   Why, anything:
An honorable murderer, if you will;
For naught did I in hate, but all in honor.   295

LODOVICO
This wretch hath part confessed his villainy.
Did you and he consent in Cassio's death?

OTHELLO   Ay.

CASSIO   Dear general, I never gave you cause.

OTHELLO
I do believe it, and I ask your pardon.   300
Will you, I pray, demand that demi-devil
Why he hath thus ensnared my soul and body?

IAGO
Demand me nothing. What you know, you know.
From this time forth I never will speak word.

LODOVICO   What, not to pray?   305

GRATIANO   Torments will ope your lips.

OTHELLO   Well, thou dost best.

ORIGINAL

LODOVICO	Where is this hasty and most unlucky man?
OTHELLO	You are describing Othello. That's me.
LODOVICO	Where is that snake? Show me Iago.
OTHELLO	I look at his devil's feet, but it is only a story that devils have cloven hooves. If you are really Satan, I can't kill you. *[OTHELLO stabs IAGO.]*
LODOVICO	Disarm Othello. *[Guards take OTHELLO's sword.]*
IAGO	You cut me, but I am still alive.
OTHELLO	I am glad you survived. I would rather you live with what you have done. It seems to me preferable to die.
LODOVICO	Othello, you once were a good man, tricked by an evil villain. How can people understand the change in you?
OTHELLO	People can say anything. You might call me a respectable wife-killer. I did nothing out of vengeance. I acted out of honor.
LODOVICO	Iago has partly confessed his conniving. Did you plot with him to murder Cassio?
OTHELLO	Yes.
CASSIO	General Othello, I gave you no reason to ambush me.
OTHELLO	I believe you and I beg your forgiveness. Will you ask that cursed Iago why he thought up this wretched plot?
IAGO	Don't ask me anything. I won't tell you anything more. From now on, I will say nothing.
LODOVICO	You won't even pray for forgiveness?
GRATIANO	In hell, you will cry out in torment.
OTHELLO	Perhaps you are right to say nothing more about your crimes.

ACT V

TRANSLATION

LODOVICO	Sir, you shall understand what hath be fall'n,
	Which, as I think, you know not. Here is a letter
	Found in the pocket of the slain Roderigo;
	And here another. The one of them imports 310
	The death of Cassio to be undertook
	By Roderigo.

OTHELLO   O villain!

CASSIO   Most heathenish and most gross!

LODOVICO	Now here's another discontented paper
	Found in his pocket too; and this, it seems, 315
	Roderigo meant t'have sent this damned villain;
	But that, belike, Iago in the nick
	Came in and satisfied him.

OTHELLO   O thou pernicious caitiff!—
How came you, Cassio, by that handkerchief
That was my wife's?   320

CASSIO   I found it in my chamber;
And he himself confessed but even now
That there he dropped it for a special purpose
Which wrought to his desire.

OTHELLO   O fool! fool! fool!

CASSIO	There is besides in Roderigo's letter,
	How he upbraids Iago that he made him 325
	Brave me upon the watch; whereon it came
	That I was cast; and even but now he spake,
	After long seeming dead—Iago hurt him,
	Iago set him on.

LODOVICO	You must forsake this room and go with us. 330
	Your power and your command is taken off,
	And Cassio rules in Cyprus. For this slave,
	If there be any cunning cruelty
	That can torment him much and hold him long,
	It shall be his. You shall close prisoner rest 335
	Till that the nature of your fault be known
	To the Venetian state. Come, bring away.

LODOVICO	I want you to understand an aspect of the plot that is unknown to you. Here is a letter taken from the pocket of Roderigo, who is dead. And here is another letter. One of them explains that Roderigo intended to kill Cassio.
OTHELLO	Oh rogue!
CASSIO	What a flagrant, savage killer!
LODOVICO	And here's another letter found in Roderigo's pocket. It appears that Roderigo meant to mail it to Iago. It seems that Iago rushed in and killed Roderigo.
OTHELLO	You wicked wretch! Cassio, where did you get Desdemona's handkerchief?
CASSIO	I found it in my room. Iago confessed that he left it there as part of his plot.
OTHELLO	Oh, I am a fool!
CASSIO	Roderigo stated in his letter that Iago made him assault me on guard duty. The purpose was to cause me to lose my promotion. Even though Roderigo is dead, his letter proves that Iago struck him. Iago led him to the ambush.
LODOVICO	Othello, you must leave the castle in our custody. I dismiss you from governing Cyprus. Cassio has taken your place. As for Iago, we will torture him by any means that keeps him alive to suffer. Othello, you will be held under maximum security until the Venetian government decides your punishment. Bring the prisoners.

ACT V

TRANSLATION

OTHELLO	Soft you! a word or two before you go.
	I have done the state some service, and they know't.
	No more of that. I pray you, in your letters, 340
	When you shall these unlucky deeds relate,
	Speak of me as I am. Nothing extenuate,
	Nor set down aught in malice. Then must you speak
	Of one that loved not wisely, but too well;
	Of one not easily jealous, but, being wrought, 345
	Perplexed in the extreme; of one whose hand,
	Like the base Judean, threw a pearl away
	Richer than all his tribe; of one whose subdued eyes,
	Albeit unused to the melting mood,
	Drop tears as fast as the Arabian trees 350
	Their med'cinable gum. Set you down this.
	And say besides that in Aleppo once,
	Where a malignant and turbaned Turk
	Beat a Venetian and traduced the state,
	I took by th' throat the circumcised dog 355
	And smote him—thus. *[He stabs himself]*
LODOVICO	O bloody period!
GRATIANO	All that's spoke is marred.
OTHELLO	I kissed thee ere I killed thee. No way but this,
	Killing myself, to die upon a kiss.
	[He falls upon the bed and dies]
CASSIO	This did I fear, but thought he had no weapon; 360
	For he was great of heart.
LODOVICO	*[To IAGO]* O Spartan dog,
	More fell than anguish, hunger, or the sea!
	Look on the tragic loading of this bed.
	This is thy work. The object poisons sight;
	Let it be hid. Gratiano, keep the house, 365
	And seize upon the fortunes of the Moor,
	For they succeed on you. To you, lord governor,
	Remains the censure of this hellish villain,
	The time, the place, the torture. O, enforce it!
	Myself will straight aboard, and to the state 370
	This heavy act with heavy heart relate. *[Exeunt]*

ORIGINAL

OTHELLO	May I have a few words before we go. I have been useful to Venice and the people know it. Say no more about my military service. When you write to Venice about me, tell the truth about my crimes. Make no excuses; say nothing out of spite against me. Tell the Venetians that I am guilty of loving Desdemona well, but foolishly. Describe me as a person not easily turned to jealousy, but, when tricked, I went to extremes of vengeance. I am like the ignorant Judas, who betrayed Jesus, a jewel more valuable than Judas's entire nation. I am unaccustomed to weeping, yet I drop tears like the gum trees of Arabia. Write down what I am saying. And add that, when an evil Turk beat a Venetian once in Aleppo, Syria, and betrayed Venice, I seized the worthless dog by the throat and killed him like this. *[OTHELLO stabs himself.]*
LODOVICO	A violent conclusion!
GRATIANO	Othello has ruined all his words.
OTHELLO	I kissed you, Desdemona, before I strangled you. My only choice for destroying you is to kill myself. *[He collapses on the bed near DESDEMONA and dies.]*
CASSIO	I was afraid he would commit suicide, but I didn't know he was armed. He was too great-hearted to go on living.
LODOVICO	*[LODOVICO turns to IAGO.]* You sneaking bloodhound, you are more dangerous than suffering, starvation, or drowning! Look at this couple lying slain on the bed. You caused these deaths. I can't stand to look at the loss. Cover the bodies. Gratiano, this house and Othello's wealth belong to you. To you, Governor Cassio, I leave the job of torturing Iago. Carry it out! I will return to Venice and relate these sorrowful events. *[They depart.]*

ACT V

TRANSLATION

Questions for Reflection

1. Describe the views and experiences with loyalty to one mate in these female characters:

- the courtesan Bianca
- the deserted Barbary
- Brabantio's wife
- the cynical maid Emilia
- Othello's mother
- Desdemona, the self-sacrificing bride.

Why does Desdemona compare her own behavior to that of her mother? How does Shakespeare create irony out of Emilia's faithfulness and advice to Desdemona as compared to Othello's mistreatment of his bride?

2. What are the details of the two planned street incidents? What elements are beyond the control of Iago? of Montano? of Cassio? of Othello? of Roderigo? How do Iago and Cassio benefit from the second street fight, which occurs in the dark?

3. Which lines from the play stress the physical elements of Othello's race? What is a Moor? At what dramatic points do characters refer to the protagonist as "black," "thicklips," "sooty bosom," and "the Moor" rather than "general" or "Othello"?

4. How would you contrast the Duke and Brabantio in their trust in Othello? Why does the Duke dismiss Brabantio's charge of witchcraft against Othello? How were accused sorcerers punished in Othello's day? How does the Duke's comment about his own daughter compliment Othello and Desdemona?

5. Describe Desdemona's relationships with her father, uncle, and husband and with Cassio, Iago, and dinner guests. How does she manage the demands of court life as a governor's wife? How does domestic violence intrude on the surface gentility at the castle?

6. Why does Othello admit to loving too much? Is he more faithful to Desdemona or to the ideal of the faithful wife? How does excessive

affection translate into a murderous rage? Why does he value his need for justice over understanding, trust, or forgiveness of his young bride? Why does he give Desdemona an opportunity to repent of her sins before she dies? Why does Othello absorb Iago's judgmental malice into his own spirit?

7. What are the state privileges that Othello acquires through military skill and loyalty to Venice? How does Othello's prestige lessen Brabantio's senatorial influence over the Duke? Why does Gratiano inherit everything that Othello and Desdemona own?

8. How does Shakespeare present the causes of jealousy? How does a guilty conscience contribute to Othello's final rash actions? How does a final kiss summarize the off-kilter relationship between a falsely accused bride and a self-righteous, demanding husband? Why does Shakespeare repeat the words "kill" and "kiss"?

9. Consider Shakespeare's views on social chaos. How do the uproar on the night of the celebration and subsequent killings threaten peace in the eastern Mediterranean? What strengths do Lodovico, Montano, Cassio, and Gratiano restore to Cyprus?

10. What is the importance of storytelling to the plot? What does Desdemona like best about Othello's stories? What events in Othello's life make her love and trust him? How does the handkerchief fit into his lengthy narratives? Why does Othello only hint at his victory in Aleppo?

11. Summarize the intensity of Othello's description of the handkerchief. What is special about the materials, dye, and embroidered strawberries? Why does Shakespeare connect the aura of magic to an Egyptian clairvoyant? What traits in Desdemona do the strawberries symbolize? Why is the handkerchief a suitable bride gift from a dying woman for her unmarried son to give his future wife? What does the gift imply about women's power over marital relationships?

12. Why does Emilia willingly arrange a private meeting between Desdemona and Cassio? What is the purpose of appointing a female companion for Desdemona on the voyage and at the castle? Why does Othello suspect Emilia of lying to cover up the misbehaviors of her mistress? How does Emilia display uncommon courage and loyalty? Why does Shakespeare punish her with a cruel death?

13. In what ways are Othello, Roderigo, and the Turks outsiders in Venice and on Cyprus? What is the status of a black mercenary soldier, even one of noble birth? Why must Othello win respect from the Duke? from Brabantio? from Desdemona? from Gratiano? from Lodovico? from the islanders?

14. Predict the strengths of Cassio's governorship after Lodovico returns to Venice. Why does the imprisonment and torture of Iago place non-negotiable restraints on Cassio's rule? Predict the new governor's relationship with these characters:

- Iago
- the Turks
- Venetian senators
- Bianca
- Lodovico
- the Duke

15. Compare messages, proclamations, and letters as the impetus to violent scenes. Why does the Duke insist on an immediate council session? What do messages in the corpse's pocket reveal about Iago's exploitation of Roderigo?

16. Make a chart of the leadership qualities in these characters:

- the Duke
- Brabantio
- Gratiano
- Iago
- Othello
- Venetian senators
- Montano
- Lodovico
- Cassio
- Roderigo

Note the qualities that they share or lack, particularly confidence, daring, obedience, balance, and self-control. How does the Duke's advice to Brabantio about accepting his son-in-law foreshadow Othello's unwillingness to forgive his wife of alleged infidelity? How does Iago corrupt Othello's leadership and ruin his career?

17. Research the humiliation of a cuckold. Why do Elizabethan rules of chastity and honesty focus on faulty female behavior rather than on male seducers like Roderigo and Cassio? Why does Brabantio warn his son-in-law that Desdemona is capable of guile? Why does Othello's mother resort to a magic handkerchief to keep her husband from straying to other women?

18. Account for the theme of illusion versus reality. What does Othello see in Cassio's drunken behavior? in Cassio's courtesy toward Desemona? in the display of the handkerchief? in Desdemona's dying posture? in the murder of Roderigo? in Emilia's confrontation with a wife-killer?

19. Justify the recall of Othello to Venice and the promotion of Cassio to governor of Cyprus, even though Cassio has a reputation for losing self-control while drinking. Why does Shakespeare reward Cassio with choosing Iago's punishment?

20. Compose an extended definition of reverse psychology. Use as models Iago's pretense of discretion and his phony hesitance to tell Othello about Desdemona's misdeeds.

21. Summarize the tone of the "I kissed thee ere I killed thee" speech. How does Shakespeare create irony out of Othello's obsession with revenge and out of the husband's adoration of his bride? How does ambiguity of motivation enhance suspense? atmosphere? conflict? plot resolution? the theme of human weakness?

22. How does Iago manage to trick Cassio and Roderigo at the ambush? Why does Iago deflect guilt by pretending to investigate the uproar and by reviling Bianca? How do first aid for the leg wound and the call for a chair and the general's surgeon elevate Iago's importance as a rescuer?

23. Define comic relief with examples from the clown's punning on the noun and verb "lie"? Why does Shakespeare choose this word as the basis of word play?

24. Explain Desdemona's elopement, her pretense of calm at the harbor, and her need to lie about the lost handkerchief. Why do small character flaws make her more endearing and more forgivable? How does her request for another half hour of life increase the pathos of her death?

25. How does Shakespeare contrast male and female ambitions, particularly these instances:

- Cassio's wish to regain his military post
- Iago's desire for the lieutenant's position
- Othello's command of the Venetian fleet
- Bianca's desire for Cassio's love
- Roderigo's yearning for Othello's wife
- Emilia's intent to exonerate Desdemona of wrongdoing
- Brabantio's need to nullify his daughter's marriage
- the Duke's appointment of Othello to head the fighting force
- Montano's desire to secure Cyprus from the Turks
- Othello's mother's need for a handkerchief to secure her husband's love
- Desdemona's request to follow Othello to Cyprus?

26. Discuss the hypocrisy of military males who frequent bordellos, yet who denigrate whores. Explain why Othello slaps his wife before guests and why he pretends to visit a brothel, where Desdemona is a prostitute and Emilia the madam who guards the door.

27. What does Shakespeare imply about the need of husband and father to control Desdemona's behavior and choices? Why does the focus on a frivolous love token—an embroidered handkerchief—heighten the irony of Othello's vengeance?

28. How does the last scene illustrate the overall loss to Venice of military might, internal order, citizen respect, short-won glory, and international stature?

29. Describe the emotional frenzy that overtakes Othello and distort his thoughts and words. Why does Iago lie to Cassio that Othello has long suffered from bouts of hysteria?

30. How does Shakespeare use light and dark as symbols of goodness and evil? What do phases of the moon foreshadow about the action? How do calls for light enhance the question of thorough investigations and of on-the-spot judgments and punishments?

31. How does Shakespeare justify the drowning of the Turks? How does Christian faith validate a victory celebration? Why does the background of Christian triumph over the drowned Muslims sully Othello's intent to assure Desdemona a chance at entry to heaven?

32. Why does Shakespeare create so impeccable a character and demeanor in Desdemona? How does her goodness contrast Othello's low self-esteem and fanatic call for justice? Does the attitude of Emilia and Bianca toward sexual fidelity indicate that Shakespeare distrusts women?

33. How do Othello and Desdemona complement each other's strengths and weaknesses? Why does the text stress her youth and his age? her gentility and his survivalism? her rationality and his obsession? What do their deaths illustrate about mixed marriage? about life with a professional soldier? about the racism of Venetians? about tragic drama?

34. How does Shakespeare use lowly people in a drama that features a Duke, general, senators, island governor, and ambassadors? How do cast members like Turkish and Venetian soldiers, messengers, sailors, Desdemona's lady-in-waiting, pedestrians, and drinkers

contribute to the action? How does the Egyptian's clairvoyance help her transcend social caste?

35. Summarize the extremes of the medieval morality play. Explain why Shakespeare uses the triad of the ordinary man buffeted by an angel and a demon to set Othello between Desdemona's goodness and Iago's malice. Why does Othello seem more human, more pitiable than either his wife or his tormenter?

36. Why does Desdemona blame herself for her murder? In what way is she a martyr to unconditional love? to inexplicable evil? to male-dominated matrimony? to an androcentric society?

37. Compose an extended definition of persuasion using as examples the relationships between these characters:

- Othello/Desdemona
- Iago/Othello
- Iago/Roderigo
- Emilia/Othello
- Desdemona/the Duke
- Roderigo/Desdemona
- Othello/Cassio
- Iago/Cassio

Why does Iago not need persuasion to exploit his wife?

38. Justify Shakespeare's use of a storm at sea to further the plot and symbolize ungovernable human emotion. Why does he build irony out of Desdemona's concern for the groom's safety? Why does the quiet acquiescence of the doomed bride singing the willow song contrast the frenzy of a jealous groom? How does suicide equalize emotional differences between the raging Othello and his murdered bride?

39. Characterize the theme of silencing versus speaking in the following scenes:

- Desdemona's murder
- Roderigo's death
- Desdemona's testimony to the Venetian council
- Emilia's murder charge against Othello
- Othello's order that Desdemona go to bed
- Iago's command that Emilia silence herself and go home
- Cassio's need of an audience with Othello.

40. Describe the illogic of Desdemona's love for Othello. How does Desdemona seal her fate by upsetting the Venetian social restraints on daughters? Determine whether Shakespeare blames or exonerates her for eloping.

Desdemona :

Notes

— more assurance in the ~~voice~~
voice like in the song.

— desdem/spirited woman. — she is still dynamic
she has gone through
a lot!

— these men! ⎫
back to   ⎬ — find a better
the song ⎭   reason
easier transition.

Notes

Notes

Notes